WIDOWED

Advance Praise

This page for blurbs from others praising my book is held for Richard Bach, author of *Illusions*. Richard wrote to tell me he has avoided doing that for thirty years and has never requested it for his own books, and then said so much more that was warm and inspired. It was the *best* decline ever. Richard Bach who wrote the most important book in my life wrote to *me*.

No other praise received will be printed on this page.

Because *ILLUSIONS*.

It doesn't get better than that.

WIDOWED

*Moving Through
the Pain of Widowhood to
Find Meaning and Purpose
in Your Life Again*

JOANN FILOMENA

NEW YORK

NASHVILLE • MELBOURNE • VANCOUVER

WIDOWED
Moving Through the Pain of Widowhood to Find Meaning and Purpose in Your Life Again

© 2017 Joann Filomena

Published in New York, New York, by Morgan James Publishing in partnership with Difference Press. Morgan James is a trademark of Morgan James, LLC. www.MorganJamesPublishing.com

The Morgan James Speakers Group can bring authors to your live event. For more information or to book an event visit The Morgan James Speakers Group at www.TheMorganJamesSpeakersGroup.com.

Brand and product names are trademarks or registered trademarks of their respective owners.

ISBN 978-1-68350-394-1 paperback
ISBN 978-1-68350-395-8 eBook
Library of Congress Control Number: 2017900220

Cover Design by:
Rachel Lopez
www.r2cdesign.com

Interior Design by:
Bonnie Bushman
The Whole Caboodle Graphic Design

Editing:
Maggie McReynolds

Author's photo courtesy of:
Tamme Stitt Photography

In an effort to support local communities, raise awareness and funds, Morgan James Publishing donates a percentage of all book sales for the life of each book to Habitat for Humanity Peninsula and Greater Williamsburg.

Get involved today! Visit
www.MorganJamesBuilds.com

DEDICATION

For every widow who spent
that first night staring into space,
unable to believe it, unable to sleep.

TABLE OF CONTENTS

INTRODUCTION

"You never know how strong you are until being strong is the only choice you have."
—Bob Marley

Dearest Widow,

You were drawn to pick up this book because you are frightened by what you're feeling since your spouse passed away. You are so alone and afraid of being alone. You don't know how to do this "widow thing," and want to know how someone else might have gotten through the pain. It is scary to have thoughts and feelings that no else around you can possibly understand. There are things you do not say out loud, things you do not share with the world. Initially, you do not even share them with yourself.

In those first few days after the death of your husband, a protective fog surrounded you. When my husband died, I felt like I was wrapped in layers and layers of cotton and gauze, so I could not feel anything at all. Our brain knows how great the pain is and immediately protects us from experiencing it all at once. But slowly, so slowly, the layers begin to unwrap and the reality of our new world—the one without our life's partner in it—begins to seep in through the protective gauze.

Your friends check in and ask, "How are you doing?" You say, "Oh I'm fine. I'm handling this. Really, I'm okay." But you're not. Even as those words of polite conversation come out of your mouth, deep inside you is a wound so painful you could not even begin to find the words to tell someone else how this hurts. So instead you say, "I'm fine, I'm handling things." And because you cannot face your own pain fully to share with someone else, you remain alone. Even your children fall under the protection of your mute button. How can you let them see your pain when they are already experiencing grief of their own over the death of their father? You don't want to add worrying about you to their load. You don't want to add your own pain to theirs. So you tell them, "I'm okay. I'm coping."

Some of the thoughts you are having seem completely inappropriate for a widow to be thinking. Thoughts of relief, thoughts of anger, or thoughts about being happy over never having to pick up wet towels off the floor again. Maybe your initial thoughts were even about being glad it was over. You wonder what is wrong with you that you think such things. Things pop up in your mind that even shock you and make you want to look away from such dark, inner pain. You replay the last days, weeks, and months prior to your spouse's death. Did you say things that were terrible to him? Did you hug him enough? Did you remember to say, "I love you" to him the day he died?

Maybe you even lie to yourself, telling yourself that you've got this. You can organize it, make lists, cross off what needs doing. But instead you end up sitting in that chair in your living room. Just sitting. Not going anywhere. Not doing anything. Frozen in time. How can you know what to do next? All your future plans were plans that you and your husband created together. Your entire life was based on an equation of two, not one. Your planned retirement was planned for the two of you. Your retirement together. Your goals together. Your vacations together. There are no plans for you alone. So now you're stuck. You mark off days on the calendar, each one a day closer to your own death.

Because of the avalanche of emotions that suddenly take over your life, you begin to question your own sanity. I know this, dear widow, dear heart, because I found myself in that well of emotional pain we label "grief." Even turning on the radio is a minefield of emotion. Songs that you used to innocently sing along with now break you right open. I, too, have driven home from the grocery store struggling to get my tears under control while reaching to snap that song off the radio. That one big question keeps playing in your mind: "How do I get through this?"

You are sure that the only thing that could fix you right now is if your husband miraculously walked back in the door. Immediately your life would again have an anchor and meaning. You think there is no other answer for your pain but his resurrection. Intellectually, you know this is not going to happen. But because you cannot see any other resolution to how you are feeling, you stay stuck, crossing days off the calendar. All meaning in life is gone, so you remain aimless.

Deep inside, you know you want more. You have new eyes on the world now: the eyes of a widow. With widow eyes you see so clearly what the value of every single day with your spouse was. You rue every second you wasted, not connecting with him, not hugging him, not saying all the things you truly wanted to say to him when you thought you had all the time in the world. You not only mourn the passing of your spouse and what you had with your spouse, you mourn what it could have been—what it should have been.

With those new eyes, you begin to see that every day in the rest of your life has to matter more. Every day that you have left in your life should never again be squandered, not doing the things you best love, not saying the things in your heart, and not loving on every person in your life. But how do you step out from the widow's black lace veil of pain to move beyond the chair in the living room? Aha—now you see the real reason you reached for this book. Your heart wants to know, "Did another widow feel this way and live through it? Is there something on the other side of this incredible pain and fear? Please, let me read something that tells me I am going to be okay."

Dear widow, dear heart, it will never again be the same that it was. But yes, you are going to be okay. You can find who you are now and what your new story will be. In this book, I am going to share my own story with you so you'll know you're not alone and you're not crazy. But more than giving a personal account of Jim's death and my own widow journey, I want to share the people, the ideas, and the tools I found along the way that brought me into the light of my new life. What this book does not include are lists of offices to contact, financial advice, how many copies you need of the death certificate, or check lists of where to send them to. There are plenty of books and pamphlets out there to supply the lists of all the places you need to contact and papers you need. You can even reach out to the funeral home director for such recommendations. Instead, this book will lead you on your journey through your own heart.

I've not left my spouse or my life as it was over the past decades with him behind, but I have evolved into more of myself than ever. I learned who I really am at my core, and I know that beyond the flimsy curtains of time and space, Jim stands just on the other side, jumping up and down in the silly way he used to when he became so enthusiastic over something, and applauding my every step. I bet your cheerleader is still right by your side, ready to applaud *your* every step.

Grief never goes away, but it emerges as something pure and beautiful that continues to live in your heart, and yes, you can live with this. You can get through this. Here, give me your hand and let's head into the heart together. I promise I've got you.

—Joann

Chapter One

THE END

"The truth is, I feel beyond sad. I feel empty. Numb."
—**Elizabeth Scott**, *Love You Hate You Miss You*

My Story

It was 1991 when Jim and I met online in the infancy of the internet, 3500 miles apart. So it was the internet I returned to when he suddenly died 22 years later to continue to tell him the things I was no longer able to run home and say to him...

We were chatting amicably together in the kitchen, in the well-worn comfort of married life, as Jim made himself a cup of coffee. He said, "I'm going upstairs to read," and I headed back into my home office. Then I heard the thud. As I ran up the stairs to see what had happened, I could see Jim was down on the bathroom floor. I turned him over into my lap and saw he was already turning blue; not breathing and pulse-less. I dialed 911 and did CPR, to no avail. He was gone. Just. like. that. It was the evening of December 29th.

Less than 48 hours later, it was New Year's Eve and I was sitting on the living room floor next to my fire, raising a glass of wine to 2015—all alone. It was not at all how I expected to greet the New Year. I was still wrapped in that protective layer of cotton batting, the one that is the physical state of shock and that protects us from the exquisite pain of loss. Yet I knew deep in my soul that this was my year to live as if it were my last. I felt that not one moment should be wasted. Each day, each hour, needed to be lived mindfully—as if death might come at the end of the year. Because it certainly could. For me. For a friend. For a loved one. No moment should be lived without joy. Every new day is something to savor.

This changed the entire trajectory of my grief and became an integral part of my own process. 2015 was my year— alone—to learn who I was and to find joy again. This is a journey I am ready to now share, along with all that I learned along the way. It is my heart that I'm cracking open as I share my own story with you, pass along the anecdotes of other widows, and help you figure out how to step into that first year and, now that you are no longer sharing a future with your spouse, reassess your basic priorities. You will discover which of your basic needs are no longer being met and how to ensure they are, as well as how guilt and other emotions can keep you trapped and stuck.

Others have told me that because they know women who are widowed, they know what widows feel. But that is not so. A widow will rarely tell anyone exactly what she is feeling—it is too raw and too painful. A widow will even shield others from her pain, especially family. This is why I launched my *Widow Cast* podcast in iTunes and why I'm writing this book, exposing all my own vulnerabilities. I hope it helps other widows begin to open up the same way, especially with each other. That way we can all learn from and support each other.

I'd like to share more of my own personal backstory, more about the story of when my husband died, how I lost my husband. I know that we each have our own unique story. For some it was a long, drawn-out process due to a long illness. For others, like myself, it was quite sudden. I don't know that one is easier to deal with than the other. I've talked about that to groups of widows and the general consensus is that it is just all hard. But I'm hoping that sharing my story with you allows you to know me a little better and helps you work through your own story.

Jim and I met in the early 1990s. We had both been married previously, so our relationship was a mid-life gift for both of us. He was in his middle 50s and had retired very young from teaching middle school in the South Bronx. I was just turning 40 and at the end of my first marriage. It was the birth of internet to the general public, and we both were writing posts in a philosophy group online. There were 20 of us all posting and writing notes to each other in a chat room. One woman in New York, Elaine, immediately felt like a second sister to me, and we connected by private email to share our life stories. Elaine persuaded me to fly out to see her because there was no way in hell she was getting on an airplane to come out to California. She was insistent and even sent me the plane ticket. So I posted to the rest of our group that if I was going to fly 3500 miles across the country, those within driving distance of Elaine's house had better meet me there.

It turned out that 18 of the 20 regular posters all ended up driving or flying into White Plains that weekend, including one Jim Filomena, who we all fondly referred to online as "The Master." He had integrated his philosophy of "you create your own reality" so completely into the way he lived his life that the rest of us were a little in awe and loved the humor he could wickedly employ to demonstrate this. He was certainly "The Master" of his own universe. I found myself surprisingly attracted to this man who was 16 years my senior. I later had to admit, nothing is sexier than a brilliant mind. Nothing passed between us that could be categorized as flirting. Nevertheless, it was less than three months after that initial meeting that I stepped off a plane at La Guardia airport and into Jim's life. Less than a year later, we married.

Shortly after we were married—one month to the day as a matter of fact—I rushed him to an emergency room because he was having chest pain. He had previously been scheduled by his doctor to have a cardiac catheterization done, but he was dragging his feet about it. Well, on that admission he was scared enough that he was ready to go ahead with any procedures they wanted. They told him, "The good news is you haven't had a heart attack. The bad news is you're sure trying." We got him moved to a different hospital, and the cardiac catheterization was performed to take a look at his heart and arteries. Apparently it was touch and go. They scheduled his bypass surgery immediately—the surgeon said, "Well, I just happen to have tomorrow morning free." He gave me a knowing wink, which meant he had canceled all his appointments to get Jim into the operation room immediately for a quadruple bypass. The head of cardiology patted my arm and assured me they would get me another 20 years with him. How prophetic that was.

Jim was a man who took great care of himself. He was mindful of his health and walked every morning. He would walk all over New York City without giving it a second thought. So even though we always knew that he would probably pass away before I did, because he was 16 years older than I was and because of his heart issues, it still wasn't a daily reality for me. You know, you just don't expect that. Living with Jim was a little like living with a character from a Woody Allen movie— he was always dying. Maybe that is a New Yorker thing. Living on the edge in a busy city can make you very aware of your own mortality. We joked about it to the point that when he would say, "You know, I'm going to die someday," and I would say, "Promises, promises. You keep promising me."

20 years and two months later, I heard that thud of Jim falling. First I ran to look down the basement stairs. I don't know why I thought he could've fallen down into the basement. Then, of course, once I got to the basement stairs and looked down, I remembered that no, no, he had been headed

upstairs. As I was running up the stairs, I could see him on the bathroom floor. When I got to him and turned him over, he was already turning blue. I remember sitting there for a couple seconds, saying, "Breathe Jim, you have to breathe—you're not breathing." Then I ran for the phone, dialed 911 and with the phone on speaker, I began applying CPR. I do remember at one point yelling back at the phone, saying, "Listen lady, I'm crap at this! You just need to get the guys here," because I really wasn't sure I was even doing it correctly.

When EMS arrived, they came running up the stairs and said, "Does he have a DNR (do not resuscitate order)?" I said, "He has just always told me to "never pull the plug." They responded, "That's all we need to hear." They grabbed him, pulled him out into the hallway, and tried to intubate him. They took over the CPR, and then began shocking him with the paddles. While they did all this, I backed into our bedroom so they would have room. But now I was trapped there, watching them work on him. They cut his clothes off. It was very difficult to watch. I kept glancing over at the bedside clock. I knew the approximate time I had dialed emergency services and I saw 20 minutes had clicked by while they worked on him. As horrifying as it may sound, I began to think it might not be a good thing if they did succeed in reviving him at that point. I was scared for him because I knew what could happen if you've been without oxygen for too long.

I noticed that there was a police officer in the guest room across the hall from where I was. At one point, he came over to me and said, "This must be hard to look at." I replied, "Yes, it is." He was so very compassionate that it helped me take a breath. I'm not sure how he even got from the guestroom over to our bedroom with all the men and equipment in the way. I certain saw no room or opportunity to do so. It was as if a guardian angel had just appeared.

Finally, the EMS guys said, "We're taking him to the emergency room," and went downstairs. My house had been swarming with EMS staff, firemen, and police officers. They all suddenly and quickly disappeared except for the one officer, my "guardian angel," who said, "Do you need me to call someone?" I said, "No, there's really no one to call." He said, "I can drive you to the emergency room, but I can't promise that I would still be there to get you home," and I said, "No, no. It's okay. I'll be able to drive. Just let me get my things." In a mental fog, I got my purse and keys and locked up my house. I drove as cautiously as I could to the emergency room because I knew that I was in a fog. There was a surreal feeling around all the events.

When I got there, this guardian angel officer was there, and he said, "I followed you, ma'am, and you're an excellent driver," and I remember saying, "I just know that I'm really freaked out, so I have to be careful." He told me to have a seat in the area outside of the emergency room. This was different. There had been past visits to the ER, and they always let me right into the ER with him. This time they wanted me to wait outside. So I knew that things were not good. Then another officer came out with my guardian angel officer trailing him. He said, "Are you Mrs. Filomena?" I said, "Yes." He said, "This is kind of noisy and distracting out here. We have a quieter place for you to wait," and he took me back to a small room in the hospital.

That's when I knew. When they moved me back to a small room by myself, I knew Jim was gone.

Shortly thereafter, the doctor came in and said, "We've not been able to resuscitate him, and we've taken a scan and it shows no brain activity. So it is my recommendation that we stop the CPR at this point." I agreed. I said, "Of course, if there is no brain activity, then stop." My heart was breaking—that brilliant brain. The beautiful mind I fell in love with. The doctor disappeared and shortly thereafter, a nurse came and took me back to where his body was so that I could say goodbye. It was hard. Even there in the ER, with him still intubated, it wasn't real to me, it just wasn't. I was somehow calm. It was as if I were outside my own body looking down at myself and wondering why I was not screaming. Why wasn't I crying? I hugged him. I patted his chest. I sat there with him a few minutes. But it felt like I needed to go. He wasn't there in that body. I needed home.

I walked down the short hall and asked the nurse, "What do I do now?" She said, "All you need to do is call the funeral home of your choice and they will take care of everything," and I said, "Okay." Blindly, I found my way out of the ER to the lobby. My guardian angel officer was there and said, "Are you OK to drive?" and I said, "Yes, I am OK. I think I'm fine," and I thanked him. He responded, "I'm still on nights. But when I'm on days, I might stop by. But know that I'll always be watching and checking on you." I thanked him and I left. I didn't immediately question the reality of this police officer. It was only later I looked back at all the little incongruities around that officer and thought, oh, my gosh, was he even a real person? Was he truly a guardian angel of some sort? Police officer or guardian angel, he made such a difference to me on that night.

I drove myself home from the hospital as cautiously as I had driven there. The hospital was only 5 to 10 minutes at the most from my house, so it wasn't far. When I got home, I came in and I sat down in my chair in the living room and I looked at the time on my TV cable box. It had been less than an hour from the time that I called 911. Less than an hour ago, Jim and I had been chatting in the kitchen. I thought, how can that be? How can it be that it hasn't even been an hour and he's gone? It felt so odd to me, like it should have been a longer process than that for Jim to have died and for me to have been there at the hospital and come home.

I realized that I needed to phone people. So I picked up the phone and I called his sons, who both live a couple hours away. It was very hard to tell them their dad had passed away. I remember calling my sister and her husband, and they cried immediately, almost hysterically. Yet my eyes were still dry. I was still in a fog, on autopilot. I phoned my daughter to let her know, and I wondered what was wrong with me that I was not crying. The people I was phoning to let them know that Jim has passed away were sobbing, and I had no tears. I even crazily questioned if I really had loved him like I thought I did because I wasn't crying. It felt like something was broken inside of me. I couldn't understand.

On those phone calls, I told everybody, "No, you don't need to rush over. I really don't even know what it is I need or what it is I want. Maybe by morning I'll know. Please, give me a day, because this isn't even real to me yet." I really didn't want people to rush to my side, because I didn't even know what was going on with me. I could not process what had happened or what was broken in me.

That night I barely slept. I could feel my whole body buzzing with electricity. I lay on my back, looking at the ceiling and trying to understand that Jim had died. I didn't fall asleep until about 6 o'clock in the morning. At 8 o'clock my phone was ringing. It was Jim's sons. They had decided that the right thing to do was drive up to our house. They were almost to my throughway exit! I had to bounce out of bed immediately. They were maybe only 10 minutes away. I ran and got dressed, put the coffee on, and tried to run a brush through my hair before they got there. No time to think. No time to process. Just get some coffee ready for the boys.

We sat and looked at the TV. I gave them coffee; we went out for lunch, I had called the funeral home and was meeting with the funeral director that afternoon. They decided to stick around so they could go to that appointment with me and so I didn't have to go alone. But the entire day was a fog and still is a fog in my memory. I sat in the chair in my living room in stunned silence while they looked on. The clock ticked by.

We met with the funeral director. Jim had not wanted a funeral. He was not good with funerals in life; he definitely did not want one in death. He had clearly relayed to me many times over that he wanted to be cremated and his ashes scattered in the river that he used to swim in as a kid behind his grandmother's house. The funeral home only needed an hour to prepare a private viewing for us, so his sons and I could say goodbye before he was sent to be cremated. It was nice. He was in an open casket and looked so much more like himself than the intubated version in the emergency room. His sons cried a little. I did not. I still couldn't.

As we left the funeral home, they went off on their way home and I came home alone, still wondering why I hadn't cried. It was not until the next morning, when I woke up, thought "he's gone," and got ready to go downstairs that the tears finally came. I stopped at the first step at the top of the stairs and had to immediately sit down, place my hands over my face, and sob. Once I pulled it together a bit, I started down the stairs again, and I had to stop halfway down the staircase. It's not that long of a staircase, but I had to sit down and have a bit of a cry again. I continued down the stairs, got to the first chair in my living room, and had to sit down and cry. Finally, I was able to stop crying long enough to get into the kitchen to make myself a cup of coffee. It was a relief to finally cry. It took me more than 24 hours after he had passed away. A year and half later, I still find odd moments of overwhelming tears—now seemingly out of nowhere.

Widow Pass

A few days after Jim's death, Gloria called. This call made all the difference. Jim used to volunteer at the local hospital gift shop. Gloria also worked there, but on a different shift. Gloria knew of Jim, and Gloria had been widowed for almost a year. She had hesitated to call me because she felt I didn't really know who she was, but she drew up the courage to reach out, widow to widow. It was one of the best phone calls I could've gotten at that time.

Gloria's first words to me were, "Joann, you need to understand that you're in shock."

As soon as she said that, it made perfect sense to me. I understood completely that this was why I couldn't cry that night. I was in a state of shock—not just emotional shock, but physical shock. I was in shock from having watched Jim die. It was like I was removed from contact with my own body, not quite connected.

Shock takes a long time to slowly wear off. It's the way your mind takes care of you after that kind of loss. At first you are in a complete fog, but slowly, the layers start to come off and a little pain seeps in, and then a little more pain seeps in. The pain is so great, and your brain protects you for a long, long time, so it comes slowly, slowly, slowly. The fog is not something wrong with you. You are not broken. Your brain is doing exactly what it is supposed to do for you. Your brain is taking care of you.

The other bit of advice Gloria gave me was that as a widow, you get a pass for the first year. You just get a total pass on everything because you're going to misplace things, you're going to do stupid stuff you wouldn't normally do, and you just get a pass on that. If you need to dance naked in your living room with the drapes open, you get a pass on that. This is your first year.

Find whatever makes you happy to do, and you do whatever you need to. And to Gloria, I say, I can never repay you for that phone call and for the phone calls that followed, the dinners together, and all the wonderful, wonderful conversations. Gloria's husband had passed after a long illness, so she had been attending hospice meetings to help her cope. It was at hospice that she connected with four other widows who all became close friends and supporters for each other. They dubbed themselves the "GGs"—standing for "Good Grief." These ladies have been a shining example of the difference it makes in the life of a widow to hear the stories and journey of another widow. Only another widow can completely understand what this is. Only another widow can connect in that way.

With Gloria's phone call, I began the road back to myself. Eventually, as I healed, I developed the steps to W-I-D-O-W-E-D, my process of finding my way through the pain to personal growth.

Step one is forgiving yourself for the mistakes you will surely make along the way and giving yourself permission to do whatever you need to live your authentic life. It is W—Your Widow Pass.

W *Widow Pass*—Find what makes you happy and do that. Forgive yourself for the small omissions, misplaced papers, and even dancing naked. You have a Widow Pass.

I

D

O

W

E

D

Chapter Two

YOUR BASIC HUMAN NEEDS

"How am I going to live today in order to create the tomorrow I'm committed to?"
—**Tony Robbins**, *Awaken the Giant Within*

But It's My Birthday!

I recently had a birthday. This year was much easier than my birthday a year ago, as you might imagine. My birthday last year was less than three weeks after Jim had suddenly died. I was still, at that point in time, receiving sympathy cards from friends, acquaintances, and family members.

Now, getting sympathy cards after Jim died meant the world to me. I don't know how other widows feel about receiving sympathy cards, but to me, it was like getting a warm hug with every card, especially if there was mention of something that Jim said or did, or what the sender's connection was to him. It was beautiful and so supportive. But as my birthday drew closer, I began anticipating getting the birthday cards I would normally receive from family members and friends. Instead, every day when I brought in the mail, the envelopes I opened still contained sympathy cards. As it got closer and closer to my birthday, it began making me feel a bit blue. Somehow each sympathy card now began to hurt because it was my birthday, darn it. It was hard enough that I was facing that birthday without Jim.

Over that week and up to the day of my birthday, I had only received two cards that were birthday cards. I could only imagine that for friends and family, it might have felt a little weird to think of sending me a cute little happy birthday card when they knew my husband had just passed away. Of course, I don't hold anybody accountable or feel animosity about it. I completely understand not knowing how to act when someone who has just lost their husband or wife is having a birthday shortly after the event. It feels a little odd to send, "Happy Birthday—have a great day!" But really, it was what I needed. Nobody knew that. How could they understand that I needed, "Happy Birthday, Joann"?

As a result of feeling low about the cards, I went out the day before my birthday and I did something I had been thinking about for quite some time. I went to the local music store and I found a little aqua blue ukulele to buy. I figured, how could you be sad if you are playing a ukulele? Just looking at the ukulele made me smile. I bought that cute aqua ukulele with a black cut-out of a shark as the fret board, brought it home, and found music instructions on the internet. I spent my birthday teaching myself how to play the ukulele. Not that I mastered it in one day, but I spent the day playing with it, finding even more songs and instructions on the internet. It occupied me, and having the ukulele indeed lifted my spirits. Still, that birthday, I was entirely alone playing my ukulele.

The lesson for me in my birthday that year being so sad and blue was really about learning to ask for what you need. When my birthday was coming around this year, I sure did not want a repeat experience. I knew that I was going to be spending my birthday by myself again; my family is on the other side of the country and my dear best friend is a couple of days' drive away. So I pulled together the courage to post on Facebook and tell people how I felt last year when I was still receiving sympathy cards on my birthday. I asked for what I wanted, saying, "Everybody needs to step up this year and send me a birthday card, darn it! I want birthday cards this year!" Oh my goodness, step up they did. Instead of the usual four or five birthday cards that I would usually get, I ended up with over 20 beautiful birthday cards with some of the most beautiful things and tributes in them. One called me the "Queen of Amazing," which I was so touched by. It was a treasure to receive all those cards and outpouring. It made all the difference.

It took a lot of courage to ask for that openly, in public that way. It almost felt shameful, like it was scandalously icky to just put it out there like that. I coached myself on all those thoughts and feelings, and I asked for what I needed. The result was amazing.

Please, please find the courage right now to ask for what you need. Otherwise, others have no way to know. They don't know what to do for you, and, truly, they have no idea what you need. When they don't know what to say to you, they often end up saying things that sound inane. But if you ask, you will be amazed to see who rushes to your side to give you exactly what you need. There is nothing shameful about it. There is such fear in putting it out there, and yet if you don't put it out there, others have no way of knowing what you need for you to feel heard and taken care of.

This year, I knew what I needed for my birthday. Last year, I had no idea what my needs were. Fortunately, one dear friend anticipated a need. Before my birthday, she sent the most amazing gourd memorial for Jim. She grows gourds on her farm, and she paints them with real emotion and things that she is just working out in her head and heart. She selected a gourd to turn into a gourd bowl, and painted it in memoriam for Jim. She knew Jim and his relationship with the squirrels in our yard. He loved the squirrels and always kept a large package of peanuts in the shell there so he could throw peanuts out for the squirrels. He had a particular squirrel that would come sit next to him on the patio table. He named him, "Fred." Fred would even hang out with our kitty cat, although they tried to not get too close to each other. They would sniff each other's tails underneath the old Adirondack chair because there, they didn't have to look at each other. They could pretend like they were not really that close.

So when Liz sent the beautifully hand-painted gourd with the inside all decorated with gold leaf, she placed some peanuts inside the gourd. This was so touching. There was a card with it saying that the gourd was not meant to be a permanent thing. It could go out in my garden and it could slowly disintegrate into the yard with the squirrels and the flowers. The gourd sat out there and slowly, slowly over the months began to break down and disintegrate as my grief began to as well. All the emotions that had constantly swept over me began to break down.

Identify Your Priorities

If you don't have a Liz in your life to anticipate a need that you are not even aware of yourself, how do you even know what it is you need? Right now you just feel hollow and alone. All your nerve endings are hanging out and blowing in the breeze, right?

After the initial shock of losing your spouse, you begin to move out of the fog of those early days and weeks and start to wonder, "What's next?" Without answering this question, days will become weeks, weeks become months, and the months will become years. Years that you will stay stuck in that place. What will that cost you, those years spent sitting in a chair, marking days off on the calendar?

I understand. There is still the pain of mourning and the loneliness. How can you even think of "moving on?" At first, you can't. "Moving on" is not even on your radar—not after a week, not after a month, not after a year. There is that huge emptiness. You and your spouse used to have a daily routine and shared plan for where your life was headed. All that is pulled out from under you. What do you do now?

The truth is that you can't move forward with the same routines and plans—because your vision of what life should be has drastically changed. The veils have been lifted from your eyes. You *see* how precious every second is. You know how precious it is to love and be loved. In hindsight, you mourn the time wasted on daily details of life and small dramas when you and your spouse could have been building even more precious memories together. You now know there is not a moment of living to be wasted. But even with this enlightened state, these new insights into living, living big is the last thing you feel like doing. You're scared, you're lonely, you're confused, and you just hurt. This is because you used to have a structure around you that met your emotional needs, and now you don't. Not getting your needs met doesn't mean you're "needy." You just haven't figured out a new way to get those same needs met yet.

I adore Tony Robbins, and he is part of the inspiration that led me to becoming a life coach. Watching Tony work, I learned we all have six basic needs and that some of those needs are more important to us than others. Each of these six basic needs plays a role in our life. But which needs are most important to us differs from person to person, because we are all unique. So the first order of living right now is for you to think about what your priorities in life are now. They may have changed since your spouse passed away. Some are probably the same. Your relationship with your spouse fulfilled some of your most important emotional needs and now that is gone. So those basic needs are not being met. They are:

Significance

You may have a high priority for significance in your life—feeling special, unique, or important to someone else. We all like to feel that we are needed. If significance is important to you and a large part of that feeling was derived from your relationship with your spouse, this is going to leave emptiness in your soul right now until you recognize this as a need and find a way to fulfill it for yourself.

Connection

Maybe one of your priorities in life now is connection and closeness with others. A big piece of that fulfillment was your spouse. But now you need this cup filled up in other ways in order to feel whole again. Initially there is certainly more connection and closeness with family around you because you are all moving through grieving the loss of your loved one. But you want to make sure you can continue to create closeness with friends and family to fulfill that need for connection. You may begin finding this with new friends in your life, even other widows who are going through the same process of grief that you are. These can be very close new friendships and create strong bonds.

Certainty

We all need certainty in our lives. How important is a feeling of certainty to you? What does certainty mean to you? Maybe it's a sense of stability or being responsible. Certainty is a way to avoid pain your life and make sure life is comfortable. It is security. Maybe it is the feeling of being in control of your life, or maybe it is your philosophy of faith.

Variety

Variety is a basic human need, more important to some than others. Variety is a way to feel alive and engaged. It's the need for new stimuli. Travel can provide variety in your life. So can bungee jumping—how adventurous are you? Those dare devils out there trying every insane, extreme sport on the planet consider variety one of their high-priority basic needs.

Growth

Growth is the need for continued personal growth, the expansion of your own capabilities and learning. Constantly feeling the need for growth does not necessarily mean you want to be in college full-time, but perhaps the opportunity to learn new things or stretch your potential is important to you.

Contribution

Contribution is a sense of service, as well as helping and being supportive of others. This can also be contribution in the sense of supporting your family. Being in service to others is what gives life meaning.

Significance, love and connection, certainty, variety, growth, and contribution all play roles in your life. But some are going to be more important to you than others. Maybe you crave variety. Maybe you've always been the one to step out into the unknown, take that risk, and do something new. Conversely, perhaps certainty in life is far more important to you than variety. You want structure for your life, a plan. You are a "feet on the ground" kind of girl. You want to feel secure in knowing what to expect each day.

Here's how you can begin to assess the state of your needs and discover where the gaps are in meeting the needs you find most important in your life:

Create a list of your needs in your own words. Love and family? Travel? Self-care? Financial stability?

Can you look at your list of needs and immediately spot ones that your spouse played a significant role in fulfilling? How was he meeting that need in your life? What are some other ways you were also getting that need fulfilled? Now that he is gone, is this a need that suddenly isn't getting met? Realize that this is a pain point for you. If he was your comfort, you now will feel completely insecure and without comfort. You need to find a way to start fulfilling that need for yourself. This is why you want to review these, and then make your list of your top two to three most important needs. Which of the basic needs are the most important in your life?

Once you have a list of your needs, start to go through them and rate them. Look at one need and compare it to another on the list. Which is more important to you? How does the first item compare to the second—for instance, Family over Travel? Family wins out? Good. Now compare Family to the next item on your list, say, Self-care. Which is more important in your life? Maybe Self-care is a higher priority. Now compare Self-care to the next item down on your list, and so on, until you've gotten to the bottom of your list and now know which item is your #1 priority. Write that item in a new list numbered #1 through #6, and cross it off the first list.

Now go back and start comparing all over again. Family wins out over Travel, how about against Financial Stability? How about against Personal Growth? Keep going like this until you've compared all items against each other and moved them over to your #1 through #6 list (or #1 through #4, or whatever number of priorities you came up with initially).

Now you have it down on paper, right in front of you. This is what is important in your life right now. Note the "right now" part. Your priorities may change over time. In a few weeks, in a few months, over a year's time, priorities can shift, and that is okay. For now, you want to address the top two items on your list to see if these needs are being met. How did your spouse play a significant role in fulfilling those two top emotional needs for you? You may have that important basic need of yours just hanging out there, empty. You want to find new ways to fill that need or begin to focus on the other small ways it was being filled in the past.

One client told me her husband was her "cheerleader." He was always the one she knew would applaud and celebrate all the small successes and wins in daily life with her. He was the one who would encourage her, build her up, and tell her that she could "do it." In seeing that this was now an unfulfilled need, we talked about how much of that she shared with her kids to let them know. Widows tend to protect their kids from their pain and emotions. But you can overdo that protection to the point that deep inside they are feeling like you are not as sad as they are. They might wonder why you are not missing their dad as much as they are. Plus, in the case of this client, she needed to share this one thing with her kids so they would not only know something she is missing about their dad, but they would now know what it is they can do for her. She needs them to occasionally be cheerleaders in her life. She can even ask them for that. It is a role reversal for sure—but I find that your family loves nothing more than being able to step into that role for you. So who will be your cheerleader in the future? You can become your own cheerleader, certainly. But it is okay to also let others know you need this. It is okay to seek that cheerleader (or cheerleaders) in a support group.

The point is to look at your top two needs and see how these needs currently are being met (or not met). Make sure you find a way to have each of your top needs met. This becomes your mission and priority right now. You cannot run around fulfilling all the needs of others around you without meeting your own needs. It's like an empty milk bottle trying to fill up glasses. You have nothing to give if you are not fulfilled. Also consider how you can increase focus on growth and contribution. What new experiences can you create for yourself? What can you participate in? It is hard to take that initial outing—that first step out of your comfort zone to go do something all by yourself that you think you might like to try. Even if it is going to a new cafe for lunch, find one thing you can go out and do.

Whatever your top two needs are, I will tell you that you must address the need for growth. We grow or die. Maybe not physically die, but emotional death is certain without growth. So start to explore. Growth is not necessarily some huge step or class or program. For most of us, it is that first time we go somewhere we have wanted to all by ourselves. For me, it was getting in my car and driving an hour and a half to a large, elegant mall in a neighboring state. Doesn't sound like growth, but it was. It was the initial stretching of my wings when I was first able to get up out of the chair I had been wrapped up in grief. Come off the sofa, out from under the blankets, and go see the sun. It is your first step to beginning to take care of your own needs.

I cannot overstress the importance of this entire exercise of looking at your priorities in your life and making sure that your top two needs are being met in a positive way. This may not be something you have ever thought about before in your life. But trust me, you have always had emotional needs and found ways to get them met—good or bad. The relationship with our spouse played a role in meeting our needs. When you lose your spouse, you suddenly have those gaping holes in your support system. We are not looking to "replace" your spouse in some way. I know very well that person cannot ever be replaced. But you must start finding ways to meet your own needs so that you are living again. It is how we move toward becoming whole again. Does being whole again mean that you are not grieving anymore? No. We still grieve. But instead of shriveling up in emptiness, we begin to live again in a new normal.

W *Widow Pass*—Find what makes you happy and do that. Forgive yourself for the small omissions, misplaced papers, and even dancing naked. You have a Widow Pass.

I *Identify Your Basic Needs No Longer Being Met*—Find ways to ensure those needs continue to be met in a positive, constructive manner.

D

O

W

E

D

Chapter Three

YOUR GRIEF PROCESS IS ALL YOURS

"The only people who think there's a time limit for grief, have never lost a piece of their heart. Take all the time you need."

—Unknown

Clearing Things Out

One of the things I started doing almost right away—because in my mind this is what you do when someone dies—was to start clearing out the house. I immediately began going through Jim's clothing to sort out what was useable and fit to donate. It was difficult because I was still somewhat in shock, but I put the blinders on and I was able to pretty much get through it.

I was also able to go though and clear out his drawer by the back door of the kitchen, where he would empty his pockets and kept small doo-dads, reminders, and all kinds of stuff. But there were other things that I was emotionally hitting a brick wall with letting go of, like his insulin. For some reason, I could not bring myself to get rid of his insulin. I would have loved to have donated it for those who need insulin. It turned out the only way to donate the unused, unopened bottles of insulin was to pay for shipping to send them overnight with special handling down to Florida, from which they would be sent to countries without enough medical supplies. I couldn't believe there was no place locally where I could pass the insulin on. As a result, I ended up hanging onto those bottles for a long time.

As I went through Jim's things, I felt anxious sometimes. I worried about what the neighbors would think when they saw my garbage bins out there overflowing with large black plastic bags only a few weeks after he had passed. I imagined them tsk-tsking that I was already throwing away his stuff. Those thoughts brought on twinges of inner guilt. Yes, I did realize how silly it was for that to bother me. Do you see that I was projecting those thoughts onto them when I'm certain they thought no such thing? More likely they felt great compassion for me. But my brain was making those big plastic garbage bags something else entirely, and that's what was inspiring a feeling of guilt.

Then I hit an emotional wall. The shock was beginning to wear off and all the pain started coming in. So to divert myself from what I had been doing, I got hold of the book *The Life-Changing Magic of Tidying Up*, by Marie Kondo. I began clearing out my own things and throwing them away, instead of continuing to clear out Jim's things. I did not realize at the time that this was something that I was actually doing because I didn't want to face continually going through his things. Not that it was a bad thing to do. I loved the book. I loved her method. I would follow it closely. For example, on one day I would get every skirt in the house and put them all in the dining room— or every pair of pants, or every dress, or every pair of pajamas. My dining room was in a constant state of having clothing overflowing every chair, the table, and the sideboard while I went through all my things. I went through my books, and stepped through going through all kinds of categories. I finally stopped short on paperwork. When I started trying to address paperwork, I realized I was now facing both my paperwork and Jim's paperwork. Facing Jim's stuff again threw me, and that is when I realized I had been diverting my attention so I wouldn't have to face that.

The question is not so much why I was diverting my own attention from going through Jim's things, but more about why I thought I had to in the first place. It felt like I would be going against what was expected, the status quo of widowhood. The truth is, this is your own very unique journey. If there is a status quo for widowhood (which I don't imagine we have had in decades), screw the status quo! I certainly did not feel the need to dress in black and wear a veil, though Jim once described something similar in his "Hollywood" version of his funeral. He joked that I could have a funeral for him if I could line up six beautiful young women to all dress in black with black hats and veils to walk behind me as I walked behind his hearse, all wailing and crying, all of us throwing ourselves over his coffin. Very Fellini. Perhaps we could include a red umbrella and a clown on a unicycle. We laughed over that one together. Jim was always one to buck the status quo.

When you find yourself in that state where you want to clear things out, let it be a matter of your own timing. Many widows immediately start clearing out clothing. Maybe it's because we all have too many shoes and we could use the room? I don't know! But truly, in talking with other widows, they have said going through their husband's clothing was one of the first things they did as well. Other widows haven't been able to face it at all. It might be their Achilles heel, that they just can't imagine doing that. I think it is all wrapped up in our preconceived notion of what is expected of us as widows.

The Dream of Their Return

A large part of it being difficult to go through things and clear out the house is you still hold onto some little piece deep inside of you that thinks, "He might come back! He might come back any day—he might walk through that door." You intellectually know that is an impossibility. But you still have that persistent belief that says, I can't throw this away. He might need it.

Also, this is part of what precipitates what I call "The Widow's Dream." I've wondered if all widows have this dream. I know my mother had this dream after my father passed and I did, too. It was not immediate. I think it was four to six months after Jim passed away that I dreamed that he was home.

It was so darn real. He came back. I was ecstatic to see him. I hugged him. I immediately apologized, saying, "I've thrown away all your clothes! I think I have a couple of shirts down in the basement still. I can get those for you." He was patting my shoulder as if to tell me not to worry about it. Then I said, "I still have your glucose meter, so we should probably check your blood sugar right away. All the insulin is gone, but let's check your blood." By then I had let go of his insulin, so maybe that was part of what precipitated the dream that he was back. I was immediately going to try to take care of him and find the shirts I still had in the basement, and get out his blood glucose meters to check his diabetes.

When I woke up from the dream, I did not feel particularly sad because I had thought he was back and he was not. I was feeling very curious about it because I remembered my mother having dreamt that my father came home after he passed away. We all have that thought living in the back of our subconscious minds. This is part of what makes it so difficult to start to change things in the house. There are things that you may change in your house that you have no issue with. I've seen widows who go into a complete flurry of redecorating and/or remodeling. My mom did this. My sister and my brothers were a little freaked out because she was spending a lot of money having wallpapering done, hanging custom draperies, and ordering new future. I realized then that it was part of her way of working through her grief. It was also part and parcel the result of having married when she was 18 years old. When he passed away, she was in her 60s. Her entire life, she had never had a house that was only hers. She had to decorate around having four kids, so it had to be durable. She had to decorate around my father's taste as well as her own. My mom was English and came to this country as an English war bride after WWII. She had never been surrounded with a décor that was her taste alone. It amused me to see how she was redoing her living room and that it looked like a typical English cottage with floral sofa and flowing drapes. It was very grand. It truly was part of her being able to work through grief, and her silver lining in her grief now she could have that living room look exactly the way she wanted it to look. So she did.

Do Your Own Process of Grief

You may find yourself back and forth with things like that. Some things you have absolutely no problem changing. Some things you come up against a wall trying to change. I still have Jim's car here and it's been nearly two years. I've not sold the car. I certainly do not need two cars, but last year, whenever I thought about selling it, I couldn't bring myself to.

Other changes didn't even immediately come to mind, and they amused me when they finally did. I find it funny that we change things as a compromise with our spouse when we first cohabitate together and then they stay changed for so many years that we forget what our original preference was. For me, at first, it was the toilet paper. When Jim and I married, he insisted we had to have Scott Tissue. I didn't like Scott Tissue, but it was one of those compromises of relationship. I felt if it was that important to him, I could certainly deal with it. So for 22 years, I used Scott Tissue. Months after he passed away, I was still buying Scott Tissue. It finally occurred to me as I was standing in the paper aisle in the grocery store that I didn't have to buy Scott Tissue. I could buy whatever toilet paper I like! I bought a roll of Charmin and brought it home with great glee to have soft, absorbent toilet paper again. As ridiculous as that sounds, it is true.

Another example: I always have a large pitcher of iced tea in my refrigerator, probably from being brought up by a mom from England. There was always tea in our house. More than a year after Jim passed, I was making a fresh pitcher of tea when I realized I was still sweetening my tea glass by glass. I'm the only one drinking the tea; I can go back to sweetening the entire pitcher. I laughed at myself that it took me well over a year to remember that I used to make ice tea and sweeten it right in the pitcher until I met and married someone who was diabetic.

My sister-in-law shared with me years ago that after her husband had passed away, she went to the grocery store and when she got to the checkout, she looked down in her cart and burst into tears. She realized she had bought all the things that she had always bought because *he* liked them. There was not one thing in her cart that she wanted to eat. She ended up abandoning her cart, which she felt terribly guilty about and still does to this day. She had to walk away from it and leave the grocery store because she did not even know what it was that she liked to eat.

It is normal to continue to carry on the same way that you did all those years as a couple together. But slowly, you start finding your way back to what you prefer and back to yourself. Don't feel guilty when you begin to find you again. Alternatively, don't feel bad or sheepish if you still have things around the house that you have not been able to bring yourself to clear out or to change. I'm sure if I were to walk through my house with a discerning eye, I would realize there are still many things in my house that are arranged a certain way because it was Jim's preference, and that I haven't bothered changing them because I have become used to that. I'm sure I will also continue to come across things that I do want to change over, like sweetening the pitcher of iced tea. It can feel freeing to change a small thing just for yourself. The bottom line is, you get to be your own cruise director now. You get to set up the ship. You get to decide how fast you will sail to the next destination, and even where that next destination is.

Are you overwhelmed? One place to start is to think about food for one if you are now completely on your own. Some people might see cooking for one as lonely and sad. But I found it an opportunity to get in touch again with the things that I had previously passed up buying because Jim didn't like them. It has taken me a while; I'm still learning about me and remembering the things I used to love that I compromised on. I'm learning how to fix food for one. It's a whole new adventure to figure out what's for dinner. You do want to make sure you are feeding yourself well to look out for your health. I find I'm using my freezer a lot when I want something that is impossible to make in a small batch. I like a nice beef stew now and then. You have to make a whole pot, but it also freezes in portions. So you can relearn how to feed yourself and how to shop for yourself.

Take the time to sit down with a pad of paper in your lap and think about what is it you used to like to eat. Similarly, what past times did you used to enjoy that you haven't done in years? I like to think back to when I was a kid and what I did that was a real treat. It has taken a lot just to get back in touch with myself. You've been a couple for a long time. Making a list of things you want to try again like foods, activities, and hobbies, can get you back in touch with who you are as an individual.

Capture the feeling of springtime that rises up in all of us at the end of winter when we want to throw open windows and clear things out. I catch this feeling every year. I can't avoid spring cleaning because I start to feel it in my bones when winter ends. It is then that I'm ready to start going through everything in the house. Give into that and go ahead and clear out a few more things.

As you find ways to adjust, do it in your own time, do it at your own pace and know that it will happen gradually over time. You will begin adjusting your lifestyle and your household. Don't feel any guilt in any way because now it is all about you. If anyone suggests that you are lagging on the "status quo" for widows, just smile at them and let them know, you have a Widow Pass.

W *Widow Pass*—Find what makes you happy and do that. Forgive yourself for the small omissions, misplaced papers, and even dancing naked. You have a Widow Pass.

I *Identify Your Basic Needs No Longer Being Met*—Find ways to ensure those needs continue to be met in a positive, constructive manner.

D *Do It at Your own Pace*—This journey is unique to each one of us.

O

W

E

D

Chapter Four

THERE IS NO ROADMAP

"Grief is not a disorder, a disease or a sign of weakness. It is an emotional, physical and spiritual necessity, the price you pay for love. The only cure for grief is to grieve."
—Earl A. Grollman

Owning Your Grief

For what you're feeling, there are no rules. People will tell you about the specific stages of grief according to the Kübler-Ross model. I just wanted to punch people in the face when they would bring up the "stages of grief" to me. They would tell me there are set stages for grief. Some would even offer which stage they thought I must be in at that time. If I said, "There is no order of emotions when you lose your spouse," they responded with something like, "Oh, you are probably still in the denial stage."

Are you with me, dear widow? Can we please gag them all?

Kübler-Ross outlined five stages. Other models outline seven stages. This is all based on one author's attempt to categorize the psychology of grief. Nice to make it all orderly and tie it up with a bow, except for one thing: There's no set timeline for how you're supposed to feel. Your feelings go all over the place. They're so mixed up. There is truly one thing you need to know and that is that whatever you feel after your spouse dies is OK. It's all OK. It doesn't matter if you initially romanticize them and romanticize your entire memory of them. It doesn't matter if you are angry with them for dying. There are widows who lose a spouse only to find there are things they hadn't known before, like maybe another lady was in their spouse's life, and they are understandably filled with anger. You can feel disappointment. I think I felt all of those things at once. I was angry at Jim for dying. I was disappointed. I loved him intensely. I felt the whole spectrum at once, intermingled. It surely was not like, oh, well, you move from this to denial, from this to anger.

The stages of grief are whatever you're feeling. Allow yourself feel it, because it's all fine. I even went through a stage early on where I felt angry because I felt maybe he didn't love me enough. I know that sounds crazy, but I really went there in my mind. I began to feel he didn't love enough; he didn't love me as much as I loved him. It took me a while to get past that and realize what it was I was experiencing, and there wasn't any truth in there. I moved through that emotion, experienced it, and realized it was all based on completely unfounded thoughts.

Some widows romanticize what was, elevating the relationship with their spouse to novella proportions. Some days I waxed quite poetic over our romance, but generally I was able to stay in touch with the reality of relationship and honor it just as it was.

Jim used to talk about dying all the time, and I think it was because men in his family did die early. He knew he had artery issues. Whenever his friend, Glenn, came by to visit, Jim would say, "This may be the last time you see me." As I mentioned, when he would tell me something like, "Joann, I'm going to just drop one of these days," I would say, "Promises, promises." There was one time, in the kitchen, when he was just annoying the devil out of me and I got really ticked off at him about something. I can't even remember what it was, now. But I turned to him and I said, "When you die, I want to remember just how ticked I am right now at you. I am not going to romanticize and tell everyone, 'Oh, our relationship was soooo special,' I'm going remember just how ticked off I am right now!" Thankfully he had the same sick sense of humor that I do, because he found that hilarious.

And you know what: after he passed away, I remembered that moment in the kitchen so clearly. I can't remember what it was that I was ticked off about, but I can remember feeling angry enough with him to say, "I'm going to remember this after you die." I actually stayed in touch with that in the early days after he passed away because I thought, no, I don't want to over-romanticize our relationship. I want to remember our relationship for exactly what it was, because it was all wonderful. It was a spectacular relationship, including flaws, squabbles, and all the times we would get under each other's skin. I wanted to keep all of it. I wanted to remember all of it: the beautiful and tender moments, the moments of shared laughter, and also all the warts and all the down days. Everything added up to what we shared together and I didn't want to forget any part of it.

There is one emotion that always crops up for every widow in one form or another. That is guilt. Guilt is the main force that sends a widow into the romantic novella version of remembrance. Guilt comes through grief in all manner of ways.

Guilty Thoughts Invading Your Grief

Dahlia was fretting to me about returning to work after her husband passed away. It was our first coaching session, and her intent for the six weeks we would be working together was to map out her future plan for herself. But the idea of returning to work was standing in the way of any forward progress she could consider beyond that. You see, her husband had passed away after a lengthy illness, so she had already taken quite a bit of time away from her job. There was sudden time off when things took a turn for the worse and he would need to be admitted to the hospital for a spell. Then, toward the end, she of course wanted to be there with him at the hospital as much as possible. Now that he had passed on, she felt her coworkers would think that it was all over now and she should be back at work. He had been gone for exactly one month, and she was feeling guilty for not already being back at her full-time job.

I asked Dahlia if her coworkers had expressed any of these thoughts about the amount of time she had taken when her husband was in the hospital or after he passed on. She said no one had verbalized any of this. Then I asked, "Have you inquired to see what they would think about your taking more time now for yourself to recover from the loss?" Well, no. She had not outright asked anyone for their thoughts. Turns out, it was all just thoughts that she was having about what she presumed everyone else was thinking.

Thoughts are just sentences that our brain plays for us. Sure, the brain may base those thoughts on past experiences or even childhood programming. But they are only sentences, just the same. Here's the brilliant part: We get to choose if we want to take that sentence to heart or not. Most of our thoughts pass us right by without our giving them any notice. There is a reason for this. We have around 60,000 thoughts a day. If we were trying to evaluate every thought, we'd never have time to eat, sleep, drive to work, or even breathe. But when you do become aware of a thought, like the thought that Dahlia was having about her coworkers expecting that she should be "over it" and back at work already, then you have a choice. Are you going to buy into that thought? Is the thought even true?

All our feelings are a result of the thoughts we are having. You can feel certain your feelings are from things outside of you. The thing someone said that hurt your feelings, for example. But no, it is actually what you thought about what they said that vibrated down into your body as "hurt." It is what you made it mean when they said that, even though they may have meant something else entirely. So you walk away feeling hurt without knowing for sure that was their intention. Perhaps someone said, "You need to not do that." Your brain plays the sentence, "I'm being criticized *again*." You immediately feel embarrassed. Maybe even slightly angry. But their intention in saying, "You need to not do that" was to take you out of harm's way! They were concerned that you were going to set yourself up for a fall and wanted to warn you. If your brain had played the sentence, "Oh, she cares enough to show me I'm about to hurt myself," your emotional response to that sentence would have been completely different. You would feel love. You would feel cared for. So the bottom line truth is, you get to choose what you think, and that means you get to choose how you feel.

Guilt is one of the emotions I find ruling the lives of my widowed clients. In a session with Karen, she mentioned how hard it was to come home at night to an empty house. I shared with her that I had actually started to acknowledge the delightful things I discovered about living alone. I could do whatever I liked without having to plan and arrange it with someone else. I could run off at the spur of the moment. If I used bad judgment, there was no one else to berate me about it but me. She said she was so relieved to hear me say that, because she was wondering if she was just callous and unfeeling because there were times it felt kind of good to come home to an empty house and not have to cook dinner if she didn't feel like it, and to be able to come and go as she pleased.

Guilt can resurface for us in so many forms. There are not many silver linings to being widowed—there may not be *any* silver linings, but for this one: We get to learn how to be with ourselves and become independent. We can have things just as we please without the constant compromise of living with another person. There is a new kind of freedom, and that is nothing to feel guilty for.

When you first lose your spouse, you are hit with an avalanche of emotions. I'm sure you know that. There is no plan. There is no reason. There is not a set pattern of grief that you're supposed to be following. The emotions just flood through. You do not immediately recognize them all. You lump them all together as "grief." But the reason grief is so painful for you right now is because you fail to see that what is making you feel so bad is guilt, anger, sadness, regret, and all the other emotions that come tumbling down. When you can begin to sort out the specific feelings you are having and see the thoughts you are thinking that make you feel like that, you can work your way toward the experience of pure, clean grief.

Grief all by itself is a beautiful emotion, because we are grieving out of the love that we felt and still feel for our partner. Grief is something that I don't think ever goes away. We are always going to carry grief with us, and why wouldn't we want to? Why wouldn't we want to remember the beautiful memories? Why wouldn't we continue loving that person that we spent that time with?

When grief feels really ugly and uncomfortable, it is some other emotion pushing in on it. There can be thinking you should have done something differently or done something more on your part for this person or with this person. You might have guilt about something you had said to them in the past, thinking, "Oh, why did I say that? I should've never...."

You somehow think that you have to hide your grief. I know I did that. I tried to bury the grief. It can be okay to do that in some social situations. I'm not going to tell you that you should do anything other than say, "I'm fine, thank you." People don't know what else to say either, other than, "How are you? I hope you're doing okay." Just understand that it is okay to not be okay. It's okay to miss that person in your life, to savor the memories, get weepy, have a good cry.

If tears begin to well up in front of a friend or even a stranger, don't be ashamed. Proudly let the tears come, wipe them away, smile. Know the tears say that he was loved, still is loved, and is dearly missed. If you are finding yourself weeping just standing at the grocery store checkout, know that it happened to me. I don't even know what triggered it or why I started getting weepy at the grocery store checkout, but I just brushed the tears away. The girl checking me out looked directly at me and my tears, and I said, "Oh, I'm just missing someone. It's good." So know that your tears honor your deceased spouse. They are coming from a place of pure, cleansing grief.

Grief heals us. Guilt does not heal us. Guilt keeps us in a stuck place. We don't move forward in our life because guilt has us frozen in time. How to handle it? Question it! Even if you think the guilt you're feeling is justified in some way, recognize that guilt is a wasted emotion. It is not going to heal you or move you forward in any way. You don't want to resist it, trying to push it down. Then the guilt will keep pushing back until you take it out and look at it, asking, "Why am I feeling so guilty about this?" You need to allow it until you can move past it. Get curious about. Think about why you're feeling it. See if you can feel where it is in your body. Does it close your throat? Does it make your chest heavy? All of that will help you process it and move past it.

Don't confuse the feeling of guilt with grief. You might have anger. You might have disappointment. You might feel fear. Don't resist any of your emotions. You want to be able to just let them flow through. Welcome them. They are part of the process. Be curious about them, because again, if you can embrace the feelings and acknowledge them, if you can say, "Yeah, I'm feeling fear. I'm scared as hell with this!" it is going to help you process that.

Again, don't confuse any of those challenging emotions with the actual grief. They are all part of the process of moving through that period of mourning until you come out the other side. Even though you may feel there is no other side, that this is your whole life—and for now, it is—there will one day be another side. This other side will be apart from the guilt, from the intense fear, from anger, from disappointment, from any of those emotions other than grief that have come bubbling up out of the loss of your spouse. Those are what you can move to the other side of. When you get to the other side, you're not "normal" again—at least, not the kind of normal you were used to, back before your spouse passed away. Instead, it's a new place for you. You're still going to feel grief, because it is the love that you have for your spouse that passed away that creates that grief. So you will carry that with you for your whole life. I'm sure that I will and that I'm going to want to.

Remember, grief heals. Grief is love. As you work through all the other emotions that you experience, give yourself time to allow that and to allow a period of mourning with an open end. You will know when you are ready to move onto something different. I often hear people talk about the "one-year" timeframe, your first year as a widow. A lot of people who have never been widowed are the ones who think you get a year. I hear widows talk about a two-year time frame. They say they are going to get through two years and then they are going to move on with their life. It is unrealistic to try and set a timeframe on your period of mourning. You're going to know when you want to start easing back into life.

You may have to go back to work at a certain set time if you have a job. Maybe you set six weeks for yourself before returning to work, or maybe your job doesn't even allow six weeks. Maybe your job only allows four weeks or two weeks, and you're going to have to go back to work and start trying to function. With that kind of a deadline, you will need to set and understand that you need to be gentle with yourself when you return to work. If you are still struggling at any point, speak up to your boss. Let them know, "Hey, I'm going to seem really normal from day to day. But I'm carrying a lot in my heart right now and I'm still working through this." It's going to help them understand what you're juggling along with your work life. It is important that we speak for ourselves to let others know when there are times that we need a little space.

You don't want to resist all those other emotions. You want to work through them and allow them until you can move past that. Once you move past that, you are going to know when you are ready to move your life forward. You don't want guilt to then come into the picture again. You don't want to think that it is not fair that you get to live your life because your spouse is no longer living. You don't want to feel guilty for having happy moments. The morning will come when you wake up and your first thought of the day will not be about the fact that your spouse is no longer with you. I promise you, dear widow, this will happen at some point. Don't feel guilty if your first thought is something else before you then go, "Oh yeah" and you remember. It is all part of the process of being able to move on and starting to wake up to life again.

There is no magic timeframe for when you are going to suddenly get better. But you will go through your process. Remember that it is your unique process. Some widows might bounce back seemingly almost right away. Don't judge. Don't think that they are mourning less because they are able to find balance between their grief and wanting to live. We can't get inside of anybody else to know what their process is.

Also know you don't have wait to "be over it" before you start living again, because I don't think we ever get over it. The heart is still going to ache and miss the other person. But you can start to live and be happy. You can even laugh and find some joy in life. There is no reason to feel guilty about that. Don't think that you're not being sad enough in your life. That somehow you are "cheating" on your spouse because you're not being sad enough anymore. Your spouse wants you to be happy. I'm sure of that.

Even guilt arises out of the profound love you experience for your spouse. You wanted everything to have been perfect in his life and you still want to be perfect in your life for him. Release any guilt you are feeling. Grief is enough without the added burden of guilt. It's a long journey. It can be very beautiful at times—touching.

I know that grief never ends and I've chosen to embrace it in my heart, where the love that it is coming from arises. I look ahead to what my life can be right now. I've acknowledged that I want to continue living. I have some life left to live and I don't want to waste any one day of that life. That's the one thing that I think my husband would be angry at me for, if I stayed in a stuck place. If I didn't get out and watch the squirrels play, plant a few flowers, and do all the little things that bring me joy in life—he would be angry if I shut that all out.

W   *Widow Pass*—Find what makes you happy and do that. Forgive yourself for the small omissions, misplaced papers, and even dancing naked. You have a Widow Pass.

I   *Identify Your Basic Needs No Longer Being Met*—Find ways to ensure those needs continue to be met in a positive, constructive manner.

D   *Do It at Your own Pace*—This journey is unique to each one of us.

O   *Omit the Guilt*—Your grief is separate from guilt, and is beautiful

W

E

D

Chapter Five

WHAT YOU WISH YOU KNEW BEFORE BECOMING WIDOWED

"Only another widow can truly understand how we feel."
—Every Widow

Widow to Widow

This is a question I've been asking other widows: what is it you wish you knew? The answers are varied and sometimes even contradictory. But that is how widowhood is. As much as we all have in common, and trust me, it is a lot, we are also having a singularly unique experience of it. And yet, even as unique as it is, there is nothing like connecting with other widows. Only another widow knows what this is.

One widow wrote to me, "One of the things that I wish I'd known was that every person who said 'Call me if you need anything,' really didn't mean it. Several times I would call and either I didn't get a return call or was told that they were tied up and it would be a couple of weeks before they had some free time. Those calls were about leaking plumbing or needing to start a lawn mower. Finally, I understood that it was just easier to call a stranger, pay them, and move on."

I do not discount her experience with this. Personally, I found that when I put out the word for what I needed, people responded. Not all of them. But if I could screw up the courage to blatantly say, "This is what I need," people would respond. I'm sure many people say, "Call me if you need anything" because that is the only thing they can think to say to you. Which leads me to the next thing you wish you knew before becoming widowed.

Some people will shun you. You're going to get just about every reaction under the sun. People who were close to you before might shun you to protect themselves from the terrible feeling of not knowing what to say or because they cannot look into the face of their own mortality, or the mortality of their spouse. This is what you represent to them; the sudden realization it could be them. The very idea of facing someone who has just had someone die in their life is far too uncomfortable, so they simply turn away. They may not even be completely consciously aware of what they are doing. They make excuses to themselves.

I was stunned at the number of people who dropped me like a social hot potato. But it made those who did reach out to me all that much more dear to me.

You will find there are people who are loving and so special. We have a family friend who had been friends with Jim since they were little tiny guys. They were best friends their entire lives. Glenn lives on the other side of the country, but has been such a source of support even from afar. He was passing through New York a few weeks after Jim passed away and we met up for dinner. It was so lovely to talk to him because he freely reminisced about Jim and expressed his own grief over losing his friend. Glenn continues to reach out with the occasional phone call to check in and chat. I am forever grateful for his presence in my life.

You will treasure anyone who can sit down and comfortably talk about your spouse and even laugh about misadventures together.

You can sometimes get people who were friends with both of you comfortable enough to share memories if you take the lead and ask about something they did together or say, "Remember the time that we...." It allows them to ease right into reminiscing. I was amazed to begin hearing what others had to share and how they felt about Jim. Awkward conversation can turn into treasure.

Some friends may not immediately disappear, but do pull away after a few weeks. It is the sadness. They want to focus back on their own life and not be pulled into your grief any longer. Your sadness weighs on them and they have to turn away. It is for their own self-preservation.

On the flip side, there are people who are so wonderful. I even had a couple of neighbors that I'd barely ever spoken to show up at my door. One was a gentleman who lives a couple doors down on my street. He showed up with a coffee pastry to give me. He said, "I'm so sorry," and handed me the pastry ring. I could see he felt a little awkward about it. I found it so touching, especially in the midst of the stunning silence I was experiencing from many who were closer to me.

Another neighbor lady I'd only talked to a couple of times showed up on my doorstep with this beautiful apple bread that she makes. She was all bundled up because it was January and didn't come in, but just said, "Honey, I heard and I'm so sorry," and gave me the foil-wrapped package. It was only a few days after Jim had passed, and in my fog I did not immediately realize that she too was a widow. It was not until later when I walked over to her house to get the recipe for that apple bread (yes, it was heaven) that I realized she was widowed and had been for some years.

Some people were strange, but I suppose so was I, because I was still in that blessed state of shock that protected me from pain for so long. For instance, I have someone that I do not speak with very often because the relationship is difficult and controlling. Do you have someone that you find you do better if you keep your distance from? This person called me a few days after Jim had passed away. It was lovely to chat and I appreciated the phone call. But then she said, "I'm flying there. I'm coming." I said, "Well, no." It came across to me that she was thinking that because my husband died, she could just hop on a plane, and our relationship would be like it was years prior.

It was as if Jim had been in her way and now he was out of the way. I felt so offended by that. It took me time and hindsight to be able to look at my thoughts about that call. Clearly it was my own "story" about her motivation that I found so distressing. This took place only a couple of days after Jim had passed, so truly I was strange as a result of shock and grief.

I've heard others talk about helpful relatives or friends who come clear out all the deceased's things without consulting the widow at all! They truly think they are helping by just getting it all done, but this is an example of hugely overstepping boundaries. Do not hesitate to push back on anything someone is trying to do to be "helpful" when you are upset by it. If you need to go through every piece of clothing, one by one, by yourself, then make that known. If someone is insisting they are going to just "rip the bandage off" for you, you can set a boundary and say no. The boundary is not malicious or spiteful, but it is how you can say what you will need to do if they continue to take that action. You can say, "I'm not ready to have his things all gone through yet. So if you continue to push about clearing things that I'm not ready yet to sit down with, then I will have to ask you to leave." Pure and simple. If you do this, then I will do that. Do not be afraid to say what you want. If you don't know what you want, say you don't know yet what you want. But you certainly want time to figure that out!

Young widows have shared with me their pain over the loss of close married girlfriends. Suddenly these young wives feel threatened by widows because they think widows are now available again, "back on the market." Of course, rushing out to find another relationship is unimaginable to a new widow.

But if the friend is not secure in her own marriage, she may fear the new widow is going to co-opt her husband, and so she pulls away and keeps the widow at arm's length. This is going to feel especially hurtful.

Lastly it can be just a matter of friendships that were bonded when you were a couple with another couple. Now that dynamic doesn't work any longer, because the friendship becomes a couple plus one. You may have concerns about the change in that dynamic that keep you from reaching out. Don't let fear stop you from letting the other couple know how much you value their friendship. An associate told me about a friendship she and her husband had with another couple, with whom they traveled and vacationed regularly. But then the other woman's husband passed away. She reached out to me to ask, "How do I include her now? I don't want to not have her friendship, yet it feels a little weird to reach out. Like do I include my husband and bring her into our plans as a third wheel, or do I plan a vacation without my husband for just her and me?" Either works. I advised my friend to go ahead and bring it up for discussion, and tell her friend that it feels a little awkward, but she doesn't want to not have time with her anymore. Her widowed friend is surely going to understand and will be able to say how she feels about meeting up with another couple or if she would want a chance to do a "girls' getaway."

It may take you time as a widow before you can consider reaching out to friends who were "couple friends" with you and your husband. We spend so many weeks and months in a fog, by the time we realize a friendship with another couple has fallen away, it can feel too late to say anything. Don't let that stop you. If it was a friendship you valued, reach out. Invite them to dinner or say you are going to be in their neck of woods next week and you would love to stop by. They might decline. They may be delighted that you reached out. Sitting in your living room chair without picking up the phone, you will never know the answer to that.

In my questioning other widows for the things they wish they knew before becoming widowed, the number one thing they wanted to share with every new widow is that however you are feeling is fine. It is not normal—nothing is normal. There is no normal for being widowed. So roll with whatever you feel and whatever you are thinking. Cry or don't feel able to cry. Sit in a chair all day in a daze. It is all fine. Whatever you need to do, whatever you need to feel, is all okay. Scream and cry in anger. Sit in a corner and sob over the relationship you had shared. Or just plug along with life. All is normal. All is fine.

Another widow reminded me, "You will want to talk about the person that died." That's why that dinner with Jim's old friend was so healing, because we could amicably talk about Jim. But you may find that you talk about your dead spouse at inappropriate times or in inappropriate situations, because you cannot stop yourself. The need to share is so deep. You find yourself telling the cashier at the grocery store all about it— then you walk out to your car feeling like an idiot for babbling on like that to a stranger. It's okay. Connect with someone who is willing to listen and let it all pour out—all the stories and memories. Let them know you need to talk about your spouse and need a willing listener. You can also write in a journal. Let it all pour out. It's good for the soul.

You will misplace documents, misplace items, and not be able to remember which bill was paid. You'll put the wrong check in the wrong envelope. No matter how famous you are for your incredible organization, we are talking serious fog brain here. Take it slow. Document everything. Set reminders. Don't think you have it covered. I got six months out and suddenly realized I had no idea where some things were in my house!

You will laugh at completely inappropriate and sometimes even morbid things. I have not yet met a widow who had not developed a wicked sense of gallows humor. If you find a friend in another widow, you can both sit on the sofa laughing until your sides split over something that a "non-widow" would be shocked by. It's fine. We widows share a very different view of life. When you lose someone so dear and close to you, it's like having a leg and an arm chopped off; your eyes open to life like never before. Priorities snap into laser focus and you know what is important.

A widower quite simply and succinctly told me, "Life goes on." And so it does. Even when you are sitting in a daze, life goes on around you. Eventually you start to join back in on that life going on around you. It is fine. You will even laugh again. It might make you feel guilty. But know it is a joy to the one who passed. Being able to smile again and find joy is a tribute to the life you shared together. Another widow wrote, "I was thinking that you will learn how to live with the pain, smile through the tears, and that you are stronger than what you give yourself credit for."

Most importantly, know there are others out there you can connect with. The support of another widow or widows is the most amazing gift. So find your new tribe. Look to hospice groups. Look in your local community. Reach out. Even the funeral director at the funeral home might be able to assist in directing you to support.

And you can connect with me. It's not for nothing I became a professional certified life coach! You can reach me at **Joann@JoannTheLifeCoach.com**. Find my page on Facebook at **www.facebook.com/joannthelifecoach**.

So there you go. Laugh, cry, dance naked in your living room; it is all good.

W   *Widow Pass*—Find what makes you happy and do that. Forgive yourself for the small omissions, misplaced papers, and even dancing naked. You have a Widow Pass.

I   *Identify Your Basic Needs No Longer Being Met*—Find ways to ensure those needs continue to be met in a positive, constructive manner.

D   *Do It at Your own Pace*—This journey is unique to each one of us.

O   *Omit the Guilt*—Your grief is separate from guilt, and is beautiful

W   *Widow to Widow Connection*—Reach out to another widow, as you will truly understand how the other feels.

E

D

Chapter Six

HOW DO I GET THROUGH THIS?

"As we begin to see where we have been absent from life, increasing possibilities audition for our approval."
—**Stephen Levine**, *A Year to Live*

Each Day Is Yours to Unfold

Just a couple weeks before Jim died, we were in the kitchen. He was sitting at the kitchen table and I was at the sink. I said, "Wow, 2015. Doesn't that sound so futuristic? Like I never even thought about the fact that I would still be alive in 2015! How about you?" He just looked at me, really confused, like he didn't get that all. It was almost as if something in him knew that he would not see 2015. I sure didn't expect to bring in the New Year without him. I couldn't even imagine what the year would be without Jim. It was a little daunting. It also made me think, "This year's going to be just me—it's all mine. It's mine to own. It's just going to have to be my year and I'll get through it."

One afternoon, I was walking through Barnes and Noble, and a book caught my eye: *A Year to Live,* by Stephen Levine. At the bottom of the cover, it said, "How to live this year as if it were your last." I knew I had to buy it. I *had* to buy it! I didn't even care what the book was about. Just looking at that cover was a revelation for me—a message. I knew that I had to live the year as if it were my last year. I think that was underscored by the fact that Jim had died on the evening of December 29th, right at the end of 2014. It made me wonder, that year prior, when we celebrated New Year's Eve, 2013: did he know 2014 would be the last year of his life? Even if not, I am sure that Jim found joy in every day because it was his nature. He held back nothing, he went for everything and it was just his personality to do that.

So I bought the book, and yes, I would recommend it. Reading what was between the covers underscored the initial message that hit me when I saw it in the bookstore. I kept it out on the table next to my chair as a constant reminder for me: 2015 was my year to live.

Throughout that year everything that marked a little bit of celebration or something new in my life, I wanted to run home and tell Jim. When you have that other person in your life, you share everything with them and you look forward to it. If you discover some nugget of something really cool and new, you want to come right home and tell your spouse, "Wow, look at what I found!" I didn't have anybody to do that with anymore.

For example, Jim knew there was supposed to be an offer letter coming to me for a job that I was contacted about. He used to come home every afternoon, rush into my home office and ask, "Do we have an offer?" That letter finally came after he had passed away. I had to hug myself and raise a little toast saying, "Hey Jim, it came through. It came through." But I missed getting that big hug and congratulations from my #1 fan. That was the hard part. I don't know if that is something I will ever grow out of it or move through. There have been many times since he passed that I wanted to run home and tell him things.

There were times that I did celebrate things with Jim. I would talk out loud to him. At first I worried about that. I was wandering around my house talking to my dead husband, like crazy women in the movies. I wondered whether someone might want to put me away if they peeked in and saw me talking to absolutely no one. But the truth was and is, I know Jim is still around. He's made his presence felt in many ways (which I will be sharing with you in a few chapters). It comforts me to be able to say, "Wow Jim, are you seeing what I've just done. Isn't this amazing? Does this blow you away? I'm so excited!" It gives me a little bit of that feeling of being able to share with him.

Early on, it wasn't as easy when I didn't have him here to share things with. One of the ways that I found to alleviate that a little bit was to sign into WordPress, where I found that I could create a private blog that was blocked from anyone being able to view it or even find it. So I set up blog for myself and I wrote a letter to him—not that I really thought he was reading it, but because I recognized my own need to say things.

It was about a week after he had passed away. I was able to write out what I was feeling, what little disappointments there were, and I knew because I had that blog I could come back to it any time I felt I needed to share with Jim. I did come back and write one more entry for him. Eventually I came back and wrote a third entry called, "More Talking to Dead People," but this one was to my mom and dad, who had both passed away some time ago. I discovered I still had things I wanted to communicate to them. But there were no more entries past those three because I found my ability to be able to celebrate within myself, and I found that I could speak to Jim without feeling guilt or worrying about others thinking I was crazy.

So to this day I still sometimes say things out loud to him, sometimes just in my mind, sometimes completely out loud. There have been times that have taken me off guard. I was in New York City with a friend, and it was my first time back there in some time. We were going into Penn Station to catch the subway, and as I walked up to Penn Station, I saw there was an elevator going down. I said, "I'll be damned, I don't remember this ever being here before. Wait until I...." And I stopped myself right before those last few words came out of my mouth, realizing that was what I was about to say was, "Wait until I tell Jim." I knew I didn't have Jim to come home and tell about that. It was hard. This was a hard moment, even though it was about seven months after he had passed away. It was the first time I almost verbalized that to somebody else.

Tackling the year, knowing that it was going to be my year and I wanted to live it as if it were my last year, made such a difference for me. Initially, maybe not so much, because I took the job that I got the offer letter for. That job took up almost all of my time and eventually kept me captive in my house because I worked from home. At first it was great, but then it became obvious that there was an expectation that I would be available at all times and that I would work seven days a week. The company had made a decision that our management team could cover the help desk phones in the overnight hours, thus saving the company some money on the outside service that handled our customer calls. So about every sixth week, I would be responsible for the overnight help desk as well as my management position from 8 to 5 p.m. When I finished my job that evening, I was still available for help desk calls, having to log in to route work through to 8 a.m. the next morning. That was for the full week that I was working and available 24 hours a day. It became difficult to even leave my house to go get groceries.

I finally realized that I was not going to be able to move my life forward in any way if I was trapped alone in my own house seven days a week. There was absolutely no joy left for me in that job or even in my days. This was the year that I was living as if each day were my last! So I made the decision I had to leave that job. It was a real leap of faith for me. This meant I was leaving that job with no income coming in. But my position had changed to the point where it was all crunching numbers and there was absolutely no time left for mentoring and coaching the people who worked under me. That was the part of management that I loved the best. So I left the job to pursue what would bring me joy.

That is what I recommend. Not that you run out there and quit your job if you're working. No, no—don't do that. But you need to look for ways to bring you joy. Find things that will take you out of your element and live your year to the fullest. Wherever you are in the calendar year when you are reading this, look at the next 12 months as your year to live. Live it as if it were *your* last year. How would you want to spend your last year? Even if you're reading this in the middle of the year, if it's July, think through to next July. Set yourself a year, and consider how you would want to live the last year of your life. Make yourself a list. Really open up and dig into your heart. How do you want to spend that time? Then start making a way to do those things. This is important. If you don't do them now, then when? *When?* Would you want to suddenly pass away and never have done any of what would bring you joy?

Isn't it amazing to think about? It can be uncomfortable to consider, because you're now thinking about your own mortality. When the loved one in your life passes away, it does bring your own mortality to the forefront. I think that was part of the gift in Jim's passing when he did. Yes, I'm telling you that I can look back at his sudden death and I can see a gift in it. Actually, a year out from his death, I could see several gifts in his passing, shocking as that may seem. The timing of his death was the first gift that became apparent. Jim was firm in the belief that we chose coming into this life and we also chose when we're going to go. Not that we consciously choose that while we are here, living this life. It may be something we even decided before we were born into this life. We may not consciously be aware of our choice, but we absolutely choose our time of passing. He chose his passing at the very end of a year, so that I would bring in a New Year on my own and have that whole year stretching out in front of me as my year to live. I truly think if he had passed away at a different time, I might not have seen it that way and missed out on major personal transformation.

But it doesn't matter, really, at which point in time you stand now. You can look at the next 12 months stretching out in front of you and ask yourself, how would you want to live those 12 months if they were going to be your last—and what are you waiting for? What are you waiting for? Go get that life that you want. Start finding some joy again. There's no guilt in feeling joy in widowhood. We do continue to grieve. We do continue to feel that pain and that loss. But it doesn't mean that we are not allowed to feel joy again. Even just looking out the window and seeing a couple of squirrels wrestling around under my oak tree gives me that little moment of lift. That little moment of joy.

So tomorrow morning, wake up, and sit up in bed. Say out loud, "Thank you, thank you, thank you; I have another whole day to explore." Let your feet hit the floor and feel a little bit excited about having a whole day in front of you to do something that will bring joy to you.

Finding Gratitude

Having trouble finding the gratitude in your heart to thank the world when you wake up in the morning? It may come to you in ways you don't expect. For example, at one point, I decided to spend a little visualization time to see what I'd be doing if I suddenly had millions of dollars. My intent was to put that creating energy out there for some good cash flow into my life. I devised this as my own "abundance meditation," but you'll soon see it transformed into a very different thing.

In my meditation, I had millions of dollars so I could do whatever I wanted to do and have anything I wanted. As I visualized having millions, my first desire was to travel. In my mind's eye, I was traveling to see family and looking up people from my past that I would love to connect with again. But the intention began to morph. I was traveling to go see various people to thank them for the part they've played in my life. Some I was just forgiving, some I was both forgiving and thanking: family, former employers. I was even seeing Glenn out in California to thank him for being a friend to Jim because I began to understand that Jim must have been a pretty neglected kid and his friends as a kid were so important to him.

I opened my eyes and started laughing—both because it was such an unexpected turn and because I realized immediately that I don't have to be a millionaire to do this. Sure, I can't just take off and travel the planet to go find all these people, but I can write a few cards out. I'll have to try that creative visualization to create some cash another time. Apparently, gratitude was something closer to my heart.

That very day, I started writing cards, some to people I haven't even seen in decades, to thank them for whatever role they played in my life and who I have turned out to be. That first day, I wrote ten thank you cards. It felt like something really big and powerful. It felt in my soul like taking that action was moving mountains that I was not consciously aware of yet. Those mountains may have only been within me, but I was moving them just the same. There were a few on my list who were tough to do. But I finally got to them.

You might want to try your own gratitude visualization. Sure, you can have anything you want, but now you also have the time and the means to go find the people who have played a role in your life, no matter how large or small. You get to drive or fly to where they are in your visualization and thank them. Forgive them if that is in order. When you open your eyes again, your entire vibration will have changed. Your heart will be full.

W   *Widow Pass*—Find what makes you happy and do that. Forgive yourself for the small omissions, misplaced papers, and even dancing naked. You have a Widow Pass.

 I   *Identify Your Basic Needs No Longer Being Met*—Find ways to ensure those needs continue to be met in a positive, constructive manner.

D   *Do It at Your own Pace*—This journey is unique to each one of us.

O   *Omit the Guilt*—Your grief is separate from guilt, and is beautiful

W   *Widow to Widow Connection*—Reach out to another widow, as you will truly understand how the other feels.

 E   *Each Day*—Live each day as if this year is your last year to live. Find joy in every day, no matter how small.

D

Chapter Seven

WHEN GRIEF IGNITES PERSONAL GROWTH

"You feel good not because the world is right, but your world is right because you feel good."
    —**Dr. Wayne W. Dyer**, *The Power of Intention: Learning to Co-create Your World Your Way*

Get into the Flow of Intention

C an widowhood be a gift? In my eyes, there is a gift in everything—even when we cannot see it. I have spoken before about the gift Jim gave me in passing away right before the dawning of a new year. I surely did not see it that way when he died. It was much farther along that journey before I was able to look back and realize that having New Year's Eve happen right after he died played a part in how I approached my grief and in my journey of discovering what my life was going to be as a widow. There was another gift that came in widowhood, and that was learning about myself. I embarked on a journey that I am sure I would not have undertaken if Jim was still alive. Clearly my life would be very different if he had not passed away.

About seven or eight months in, I confess I was beginning to waiver in my resolve to make the most out of every moment of every day. It was beginning to become difficult to want to get out of bed in the morning. I was dragging through my days. Then what I can only describe as a divine intervention came to me: I realized that it was time to become a life coach.

This turned my world around. I had taken that new job shortly after Jim passed away that started out pretty great. But then everything changed, and I was no longer doing what I loved. Small wonder my spirits had begun flagging. Now it is such a passion for me to be able to focus on life coaching others and to share the experience and lessons I've learned over my lifetime.

I have always known that our thoughts create the very reality around us. When Jim and I met online, it was in a group discussion about this very thing. Together we pored over materials and studied all the philosophers. He taught me Greek and Roman mythology and how it pertains to our daily life. He shared Carl Jung and James Hillman. When I said I was going to study psychology at Penn State, he insisted it would only muddy these truths. At the time, Penn's psychology program was a very traditional curriculum, not yet bringing in the study of neuroscience, which culminated in what I already know. Our thinking creates our reality, as surely as the sun rises and the moon sets.

I set out researching schools where I could become certified as a life coach. Yes, it is still a field in which I could have just hung out a shingle for "life coach" and started a business. Believe me, many have. But I felt that to be unethical. I wanted a solid grounding and certification. So my search began. Many schools were stuck basically 20 years in the past in psychology and counseling. I wanted no part of that. Many were focused more on business coaching. I finally found my school and mentor, Brooke Castillo of The Life Coach School, out in California. She taught a model of coaching that was completely in sync with my own beliefs and experiences. It demonstrated exactly how our thoughts create our emotions, and everything we do and don't do is because of how we feel or how we do not want to feel. Those actions create results in our life that will inevitably prove out the thought in our brain that set those wheels into motion. The next class cycle was scheduled for September, but September was sold out and I could not get in. I was placed on a wait list.

I kept in touch with the school, insisting that I was coming in September. But the time went by without anything opening up, right into the very week that the new class cycle was starting. I was sitting outside my gynecologist's office, waiting for that yearly visit. Dr. Wayne Dyer had passed away shortly before, and his family generously made all his eBooks available for 99 cents because they felt it was his wish to reach as many people as possible. I was reading his book, *The Power of Intention,* in which he described intention as being a spiritual flow we could tap into. I did a short exercise that he described in the book. I mean, what else is there to do when you are discreetly sitting outside the gynecologist's office?

Dr. Dyer wrote about growing up in New York City and riding the subway with his mom. They would get on the subway, and she would reach up to hold onto one of the leather strap handles that were still in subway cars back then. Because Wayne was little and couldn't reach a strap handle, he would have to sit on the bench seat. He used to pretend that he could float up and grab onto a strap handle. As an adult, he used the image of the leather strap handle to remind himself to get back to intention as a spiritual flow as opposed to something inside our head. He described imagining leather strap handles floating by just above your head. These handles are attached to the subway of intention. You can let go of ego and let go of where you think you "should" be headed and how that "should" happen, and then just float up and grab onto one of those strap handles over your head. Allow the powerful spiritual flow of intention take you to where you need to be. You surrender to it, you lighten up. So I got all my preconceived notions of what was supposed to happen for me out of the way and just grabbed onto that flow of intention to let it take me where I needed to be.

When I got home after my appointment, I was putting my key into my door when my cell began ringing. It was The Life Coach School saying, "This never happens. But one of our students has had an emergency and cannot come. So we have an opening if you can be here tomorrow." Tomorrow? I was on the east coast, it was about 4:30 p.m. and the school was on the west coast. It was crazy. Insane. But I knew it was meant to be. Yes, I made it. I packed a case, jumped on a flight across the country, and got there at 2:30 a.m. before the first morning of classes.

Dare to Dream

My new direction for growth had been set. I was doing the personal work of processing my own emotions. I had been extensively coached during the two weeks I was out in California. As a result, I returned home wanting to hit the ground running every morning. It is when you find that sense of purpose again that your life begins to take shape. You find some excitement in starting your day, every day. Even if you just begin to schedule a few things here and there so there is something to constantly look forward to. For heaven's sake, you can even get hooked on a TV show to look forward to! I do not miss Sunday nights in front of my TV with *The Walking Dead* or *Game of Thrones*.

The certification process for life coaching was very exciting. But at the same time, I don't think I've ever felt so completely alone. But that's how it is, starting up a solo business. Every day is exciting. Yes, there are times of depression and self-doubt creeps in. There are high highs and low lows. But you know what? It is living. All of it. No matter the size of the new endeavor you take on, you can start to be alive again.

I have a set of postcards that a dear friend sent to me early in 2015 called "Women and the Hourglass." They are crayon drawings of women in various yoga poses. They say, "One day she woke up and decided to be happy." "One day she woke up and decided to color outside of the lines." "One day she knew she must follow her heart." "One day she opened her mind to all the possibilities." The artist for these cards has since done many, many more. One I love is "One day she woke up and decided she was beautiful." If you are one of my podcast listeners, you know I love "One day she woke up and infused joy into her life."

I taped the four postcards up on the wall over my bed so that they would watch over me every night as I slept, and I would wake up and see the ladies each morning. Each morning I see "One day she woke up and decided to be happy," and I say out loud, "Thank you, thank you, thank you for another beautiful day on this planet." I make sure I am getting out of my bed in a state of gratitude for being alive. So even on days when I do not get out of my house, I am so excited about what I write, podcast, and share. When I learn something new I can share with my widow clients or in my research on the psychology of eating and weight loss, I cannot wait to reach out with the new information.

Don't let your sadness carve itself into your brain as a permanent neural pathway. Neuroscience has quite complex explanations for this. But I am not a specialist in that field, so will keep my explanation simple. Neural pathways are created in our brains through repetition and habit. A neural pathway could be created through a traumatic experience. Once that pathway is there, the brain defaults to it. This is the kind of thought that plays in your head all the time—a thought that just always comes up for you. It is a deep neural pathway.

But know that if sadness has become a default neural pathway in your brain, your brain is able to be remolded at will. You can create *new* pathways in your brain—pathways of joy. If you are willing to open your mind to any and all possibilities, there are many avenues open before you. I've seen many widows find fitness, and just like that, their entire life changes, revolving around the joy of working out or running. Other widows might become founders of support-groups for support. It is what begins to give them direction and meaning in their life. Maybe you find you want to write, or paint, or do a play. Whatever makes that little vibration of excitement begin inside of you, grab it. Then go *all in*, 100%. Commit to it like it is a matter of life or death. Because it just may be a matter of life: living fully and joyfully. It will make that state of living with joy a new neural pathway.

Posttraumatic Growth

When I started interviewing widows whose loss was around four or five years ago, I found there was a consistent posttraumatic stress disorder reaction they experienced a few years into the widow journey. They initially walked through that first year thinking, "I'm okay. I'm doing fine." Some even dove directly into huge projects as a means to distract themselves from the immediate pain of loss, thus effectively delaying the entire processing of emotions.

It was a revelation to me that we, as widows, can experience PTSD (posttraumatic stress disorder) because the loss of our spouse is so shocking, painful, and even disorienting. I had always associated PTSD with soldiers returning from terrible war, having witnessed such terrible things, and cases of other extreme trauma. I equated it to the experience of *physical* trauma, but it also comes from *psychological* trauma. It did not occur to me that this is something that was happening to all of us. But it surely was and still is in the sense that you will likely continue to display symptoms like suddenly sobbing with no idea why you would be shaking and crying like that at that particular moment. Small things can "set you off" into sobs of grief. This goes right along with the fact that you physically and mentally go into a state of shock at the time your spouse passes. It makes sense to realize that a form of PTSD would follow.

But out of this horrible shock and PTSD is the potential for amazing personal growth. So the first time I heard the phrase posttraumatic *growth*, it just stopped me in my tracks. I wanted to jump up and down and say, "That is it. That is exactly it." I think this growth comes to us in many ways or stages. Often, we dive into something as a distraction from our grief and the posttraumatic stress, and distracting ourselves from it allows us to carry on. There is nothing wrong with that. It is what some of us need to be able to even function at that point. For example, I started a new job just a couple of weeks after Jim died, glad to have an income and something else to focus on, even though I ended up leaving that job seven months later when I realized it was not a good fit for me.

It is when we stop distracting ourselves from our grief and begin accepting the emotions of our grief that post-traumatic stress begins to show itself. Have you found yourself crying more and more easily? Certain commercials on TV can just do me in! Fortunately, when we lean into and move through this posttraumatic stress, growth accelerates.

For widows, this posttraumatic growth is not something we have to consciously reach to achieve. You cannot avoid the initial growth. Right from day one, you have to begin to reach deep inside to find the strength to deal with daily life. It is from there that you begin to find that you are stronger than you ever thought you were. At first you don't see it because you feel like a wet kitten. But honestly, the point comes when you realize how strong you are. Jim made me strong and independent. In my relationship with Jim, I became a better person. That did not go away when he fell dead at my feet. I am to this day a better, stronger person for having been in relationship with him. But how I grow now, going forward, is what is truly amazing.

Yes, the death of a spouse changes your life completely— but the growth stage *really* changes you. Even after only 16 months as a widow, you can feel that you are a different person than you were just 16 months ago. The shape of your life may be very different than it was then. It is through the retelling and re-experiencing of your story for once and for all –and even having someone take you through your thoughts and struggle with the passing of your spouse—that you can move from the PTSD stage of widowhood into posttraumatic growth.

I know so many of you are struggling just to bounce back from your loss. But there is really no going back to how we were prior to our loss—we all know this. When you suffer the trauma of your spouse dying, there is no bounce-back like there can be for the physical trauma of injury that can heal over time. Our lives are forever changed. But you can actually bounce *forward*.

You bounce forward to a stronger you and a new life. You never "let go" of your spouse or your past as many around us imply we need to do. They want to help you, but having not suffered the same kind of loss, they really have no idea how to help you. You carry all that with you as you bounce forward into your new life and your new abilities.

Do you have interests that you may have back-burnered over the years, but now find waiting like dusty old books on a shelf? Take them down, brush them off, and open them back up again to find great joy in those things again. As you find the time and energy to spend on them, you begin to grow forward. Your great loss becomes the basis for great change. I've talked before about how, upon the death of our life partner, our eyes are immediately opened to a very deep appreciation for life and the need to savor every day. We have a view of the world like never before—similar to that of those who've had near-death experiences. We get that gift in the passing of our spouse. We know how damn precious every minute is. And it is through those new eyes that we begin to tap into an inner strength beyond anything we ever knew we had and begin to grow forward. We develop a deeper and more meaningful relationship with ourselves and become a new and stronger version of ourselves.

I am Joann 2.0.

In Stephen Joseph's *What Doesn't Kill Us: The New Psychology of Posttraumatic Growth,* he says, "Trauma is not an illness to be helped by a doctor." I feel so vindicated! I have been saying all along that being a widow experiencing grief is *not* a pathology. It infuriates me when others treat a widow's grief as something that needs medication or a shrink. No, no, no. This is something natural that you are moving through, and you can begin to write your personal story into one of survivor and even heroic outcomes. You can begin posttraumatic growth.

This is the paradigm that I operate within and the way I approach life coaching with widows. Together we begin to rewrite that narrative of what has happened to you, and you begin to move from your place of distracting yourself from your grief into that place where you begin to grow into your new life. You can let go of all the twinges of guilt at moving forward as a stronger and better version of yourself, and feel proud knowing your spouse is probably looking down on this amazing, amazing woman and applauding. You are letting go of your sad story and writing your powerful, phenomenal new story.

I remember my mom telling her widow story over and over again, to every stranger she would encounter, even the checker at the grocery. I was so embarrassed for her and would tell her, "Mom, don't tell every stranger!" I didn't understand then that she was stuck in her story. If only she had reached out to someone for support, she could have gone through her story one last time and then begun rewriting her story.

So ask yourself, now what? Do I stay in a place of distraction and sadness, or can I now begin to move into posttraumatic growth? Your new solo status is not something you would have chosen, not by any means. But it *is* an opportunity to become stronger. It is the opportunity to become more *yourself* than you ever were. So let this become your story: how you felt in the early days, and how you move through your first year, and how you find tremendous inner strength. *You* are amazing—every one of you reading this. You have no idea how amazing you are, but look at what you are surviving. Look at the life you get to now build, just for *you*. The very thought may even now bring up feelings of guilt. Perhaps you think you cannot possibly think about a life without your spouse. But you will. You can. You are not "letting go" of them. You are becoming more of who you are. I know this is true; I've coached many widows past the emotional pain and into the beauty of pure grief, helped them get a clear vision of what is next. They experienced the personal growth that working through the emotions can produce. You can, too.

W   *Widow Pass*—Find what makes you happy and do that. Forgive yourself for the small omissions, misplaced papers, and even dancing naked. You have a Widow Pass.

I   *Identify Your Basic Needs No Longer Being Met*—Find ways to ensure those needs continue to be met in a positive, constructive manner.

D   *Do It at Your own Pace*—This journey is unique to each one of us.

O   *Omit the Guilt*—Your grief is separate from guilt, and is beautiful

W   *Widow to Widow Connection*—Reach out to another widow, as you will truly understand how the other feels.

E   *Each Day*—Live each day as if this year is your last year to live. Find joy in every day, no matter how small.

D   *Dare to Dream*—Yes, you experience emotional trauma, but this can also inspire you to reach for tremendous personal growth. It is through this that you find out who you really are and learn just how strong you really are.

Our WIDOWED acronym is complete to help you identify the steps that are going to get you started on finding your way through the pain of your loss. Remember, you have a "Widow Pass"—I just gave it to you! Identify your basic needs that are no longer being met and find a way to ensure you are meeting your own needs. Do all of this at your own pace. Own your grief and don't let guilt constantly creep in because others are trying to dictate how or what you should be feeling and for how long. Widow to widow, find connection and offer connection to other new widows. Each day should have some joy in it. Live each day as if it is your last. Dare to dream, because it is through this journey you will reconnect with the amazing woman who has been there all along, inside of you.

Chapter Eight

THAT WIDOW MOMENT

"Most people think that a widow is inhabiting some elegiac world of—it's like Mozart's Requiem Mass. You know, it's very beautiful and elevated thoughts and some measure of dignity. I didn't have that experience at all. I had one pratfall after another."

—**Joyce Carol Oates**, being interviewed on *PBS Newshour*

Grief Sneak Attack

J im passed away right at the beginning of when winter here in the northeast starts to get very cold and very snowy. The first big snow storm came, and it was a whopper. I think at the base of my driveway it was almost three feet. It was different in different places on my driveway because snow can drift, but at the lowest point it was still two feet of snow. That's a lot. It's difficult to try and shovel two feet of snow. I don't know if you've ever experienced shoveling snow before; when it gets that deep, you cannot take just one scoop to clear a spot. You have to scoop out three to four different shovelfuls just to get down to the pavement in that one little one- by two-foot spot that you're shoveling.

So we had a significant storm, and I went out to try to start the snow blower. I couldn't find a manual for it. I seem to vaguely remember, as I was going through a few things upstairs after Jim passed away, that I had seen the manual for the snow blower. But I had no idea where. I couldn't find it, and I was a little annoyed that it wasn't in the accordion file where we always kept all the manuals for everything. But the snow blower was Jim's baby, so he had that manual stashed away somewhere else. There were a number of times in the winters that he had showed me how to start the snow blower, or had it running and had me get behind it just so that I could get the feel of it. But he would immediately take it back, because snow blowers are really just big toys for big boys. You can lay money on that. Whenever we would get a significant storm, all the dudes would be out there after the storm with their snow blowers, bundled up and everybody snow blowing at the same time. It was like male bonding going on in the neighborhood over their snow blowers.

I was already beginning to feel annoyed when I headed out to the garage and the snow blower. Failed attempt after failed attempt to start it up ensued, filling my mind with thoughts that I was not going to be able to take care of myself. I could be stuck in a storm if I couldn't get help, but I wanted to prove to myself that I could be self-sufficient now that I was on my own. I had thoughts about my memory lapse in not being to remember where I had come across the little book for the snow blower. I even started to feel angry at Jim for not being there.

More and more discouraging thoughts raced through my mind, and I just wanted to sit on a pile of ice and cry. I had been warned about the time that something goes wrong and all the widow sadness seems to catch up at once. I think that was it. All that sadness, anger, and frustration that I had been trying to ignore found this moment as the chance to burst out of hiding, all at once. I sent a text to a neighbor asking for help. He was away doing something, but said, "When I get home later, I'll take a look at it for you." This was very kind. But in the meantime, I realized that if I didn't start trying to get that snow cleared, there was going to be no clearing it. It can warm up and melt a little, and then refreeze. Then it becomes more solid and ice-like. Every time the plows go by your property, more and more snow and ice is getting pushed up against the bottom of your driveway. Those of you in the Northeast know full well what I'm talking about, I'm sure.

I bravely got my snow shovel out and got myself down to the bottom of the driveway to start there first. I thought if I at least cleared the bottom edge where the plows were building up snow and got the snow cleared out from in front of the car, which I had left parked close to the end of the bottom of the driveway, I would be able to get the car out in an emergency.

So I was down there, and I was feeling pretty sorry for myself, but I was holding it together. I was trying to shovel through this snow and ice that was up past my knees. To toss each shovelful of snow up onto a snow bank took all I was worth. My "holding it together" was beginning to lag a little under all the self-pity.

It was just about that time that the mailman came trudging through the snow and he said the three words he probably should not have said to me at that very moment. It was the same words you've heard over and over as a widow. He said, "How are you?' It was all I could do to not start sobbing, right into the ugly cry, right then and there on the poor postman. I think I said, "I've been better," and took my mail from him quickly because I did not want to just start bawling.

I choked back the urge to ugly cry, the huge grizzly lump in my throat, and had pulled it to together again to continue shoveling at the bottom of the driveway when I heard a very deep voice behind me say, "So are you trying to have a heart attack too, Jo?" It was my neighbor. He fussed with my snow blower and got it going for me. Neighbor to the rescue. But my brain was still playing the sentence that said, "You have to be self-sufficient or you'll be stuck."

Throughout last winter, my snow blower became my ongoing saga. I could have gotten someone to come snow blow my driveway. But I needed to prove to myself that I could do it. I wanted to know that if a storm happened, and I couldn't get somebody to show up, and I needed to get my car out; that I could get out there and clear my driveway. But every storm that happened there was always something with that snow blower and the repeating thought that I could not do this.

Finally, by the end of winter, I had nailed all the steps it took to start that snow blower. I had memorized them. I knew them. I typed them out in a list and printed it out. At the top in large red text, it said, "Bastard Snow Blower" and listed all the steps to start it. I put it in plastic lamination and tacked that up on the wall in my garage. Now I was going to be ready to tackle that snow blower.

The last good-size storm that came last winter, I was ready, I had my list. I went out there. I was going to do this one on my own. I went through all the steps on the Bastard Snow Blower list and it started right up, which was great. I unplugged the electric starter cord from it and it promptly died. I again wanted to burst into tears. I couldn't imagine what was going on. Finally, I looked into the gas tank and it was empty. My gas can that I had handed to Jim last fall and said, "Shouldn't we fill this up?" was empty. He had said, "Oh, we have enough gas in that snow blower to get through the whole winter. Don't even worry about it."

It had been a long, ongoing winter ordeal. But it was that first time I failed with the snow blower that was my first experience of a widow moment—that moment when grief sneaks up and all the swallowed sadness and tears ambush you out of nowhere. I was angry at Jim for putting the manual someplace where I couldn't find it, I was angry with myself that I could not get it started, I was angry at the snow blower, I was angry at whoever designed snow blowers to begin with. I was sure it had to be men, because if it had been designed by a woman, there would be *one* button to start that sucker. Honest to God. It took seven different steps to get it started! Only a male designer would do that. Okay. Sorry for my sexist rant. But I know you ladies know what I'm saying.

So have you had your widow moment where you tried to do something that you just couldn't get through by yourself and you wanted to sit down and cry? Or perhaps you actually did sit down on some random rock and let the tears flow. Help will generally show up. You will eventually triumph. Knowing that your thoughts create your emotions does not help sometimes. Sometimes you need to let all the emotions come on in and sit on that rock.

What was the fate of the snow blower? At the start of the next fall, I got it serviced and ready to go. I tested it after I got it back home and I was able to start it right up. So I put it away until our first snow storm, which did not happen that second winter. There was not a single chance to get it out and see if I could clear my drive. So this saga continues. But if I am snowed in this winter, I am much better prepared mentally to tangle with it.

Be aware of widow moments and don't feed badly about it or frustrated. Just understand it is going to happen. It's like all the sadness piles up into that one moment. It can be something simple. It could be having to swipe your card twice at the grocery store and you break into tears. You get a pass. Remember, first year as a widow, you get a pass. I think we may even get a pass in the second and third year. I may be able to get a pass for the rest of my life if I can wangle it. I definitely cut myself a lot more slack these days than I did before in my life.

Landmark Days in Grief

In my coaching practice, I've been hearing from widows and widowers who are in such a deep, dark place in their loss. There is great anger, and there is great pain. They may see other widows as not "getting on with their life" and feel mad at them because those other widows present a scenario where someone is still hurting a year later, two years, three years or even many, many years later. It might mean their pain, their anger, and their depression are never going away. I cannot with certainty say that grief ever goes away—but it certainly mellows, and everyday life becomes a new kind of routine and normal for you. Still, there are moments that can overwhelm you with sadness, those widow moments. But you just have to allow yourself that moment and know that you have moved on in some manner. Not moved on as in forgetting your spouse, but moved on in the nature of rebuilding your daily life. You will be functional again. Some even find love again. I'm sure the new love does not replace the old love, but is a new chapter of the heart.

What can indeed keep you in the deep, dark place forever is how you are choosing to think about your life right now— the thoughts that you focus on about what losing your spouse means to you. Your own thoughts and outlook can create emotional pain or ease emotional pain. Remember, you get to choose. If you think your life will never be the same, you are right. If you make that mean your life will never be good, that is what you are choosing to focus on and you will give exactly that to yourself. You will experience life in a miserable state and as a struggle. This is not all positive thinking "hoo-ha"—this is about how you approach your own life. Sure, there will be those early weeks when it is very difficult to imagine that your life can be anything but this pain. But the fog will begin to lift and when it does, you want to be able to lift up your head and look at the road before you. It is full of possible paths and you get to choose which one.

Even when you've reached the point that you start re-creating structure in your days and making an effort to get yourself out of your house, even if just for a walk, there are always going to be landmark days that come across the calendar with all the memories those days carry and the sweet pain of beautiful memories coupled with the pain of loss returns. Expect them. Celebrate them, even if it is in just some small gesture. Christmas, Fourth of July, anniversaries, birthdays. A couple of widows I've coached have grandchildren who were born after the loss of their spouse. How bittersweet to welcome a beautiful child into the world and yet feel that their spouse should be there to share in that joy! Maybe those widows even feel cheated a bit that they are experiencing this without their spouses. Many, of course, feel that their spouse is indeed present at the occasion. But that is not the same as physically present. Yet, you can choose to give yourself over to that joy and celebrate the new family member in great happiness.

I still get twinges over the things I so wish to share with Jim. Even little things. Even the *American Idol* finale. Oh, don't laugh and don't judge! Jim rarely watched TV. But for many years, we loved to sit together in the living room and watch *American Idol*. We would feel so invested in watching the young stars developing their talent. This season was the last one for *American Idol*. As it came to the end, they did many special retrospective segments, and one entire show was devoted to clips of seasons past. It took my breath away—like watching the seasons of my life together with Jim sweeping by. This year's contestants were extremely talented—I enjoyed watching, but kept thinking how Jim would have loved that singer or a particular performance. It tugged at my heart constantly—like a major milestone. It was like another anniversary date of one sort or the other.

These dates can be especially difficult if you are on your own or living distant from family. Many widows find themselves completely alone. Holidays when you are alone are especially hard because you do not have the distraction of family around you. So you anticipate and plan. Perhaps have some small thing you want to do to mark the day. It can be simple—but it is what you need to move through the day. On Easter Sunday, I made a simple dinner for myself. It wasn't much, but it was a nod to our Easter dinner tradition: ham with yams and even a deviled egg. I knew it would make me sad to not have a ham dinner on Easter. So I planned for it. I didn't make a big deal out of it, but I made sure I had a ham slice and yams here to fix. You find the traditions you need to hang onto.

Jim's friend Glenn referred to New York's Esopus River as Jim's personal Ganges. So it was. Jim had always said that when he was gone, I was to scatter his ashes off of a particular old bridge over the Esopus River. He was a New Yorker—he was raised in Queens and lived in New York City his entire life. But as a kid, he was sent every summer to stay with his grandmother in Mt. Tremper. The Esopus ran right behind his Gran's property, and he would swim with his cousin, Jacky, upriver to underneath this bridge. We scattered him there a year ago on his birthday, so the Esopus River could carry him back out to the Hudson River, down to his beloved New York City, and then wash out to Queens. His return journey was complete.

Yes, the bridge has been closed for years—and yes, it was a bit illegal to squeeze through the hole in the fence to go out on the bridge and scatter ashes over the side. But Jim would have loved the illicit nature of the whole thing. When I revisited the bridge on the anniversary of scattering his ashes, I did not squeeze through and clamor over the rail. Instead, I wove a bundle of Jim's favorite flowers into the chain-link barrier on the bridge, and then sat off on the side, overlooking the Esopus rushing out from under the bridge. In my mind I could see two very small boys, swimming for all they were worth against that current to make it all the way to the bridge. I laughed to myself—modern mothers would perish over the thought. But back then, it was natural to let kids run free and try crazy stuff. Jim never really stopped running free and trying crazy stuff.

When we scattered Jim's ashes, we did it on his birthday. You could think that I get a double-whammy each year. But when the date came around for the first anniversary of scattering his ashes and his birthday, I smiled to myself that I had unwittingly created a situation where I can grieve both days all on the same day. Instead of grieving his birthday each year and grieving the day of scattering his ashes, I can move through my grief all in one day. Thrifty of me, eh? Well, it just works out that way for me. I could make it a big deal—like I'm suffering double grief. Instead I choose to ask, "What is perfect about this?" and smile that I can just devote that whole day to memories.

So I felt good about sitting next to the bridge to commemorate his birthday and his ashes day. I drove on into Phoenicia. This was one of the first places Jim took me to when I moved to NYC. He loved it up here, and we would often drive up to stay a few days in Phoenicia by the Esopus. We finally bought a house upstate and moved out of the city to the Hudson River and the Esopus. So after saying, "Happy Birthday" to Jim on the bridge, I went into town to the restaurant that was a favorite breakfast spot of ours. I always used to say, "One day we have to come later in the day so I can try a slice of their wood oven pizza." That day, I sat at the lunch counter and had a slice. I walked through the town of Phoenicia and looked at all the spots he loved to photograph. It was a little melancholy to look at the views and the spot on the street where I had snapped the last picture I ever took of Jim. But I did fine the whole time until I got home again and walked in the door of my house. Somehow it all "hit" as I walked in my side door into my kitchen and I sobbed.

Have you had your widow moment yet—that point in time where you really kind of just lose it over something small, something that becomes a challenge? All those emotions I just spoke to you about in the last chapter break loose like Armageddon.

My day-to-day life has shaped itself into my new normal—into who I am now. But there are still moments that take me by surprise—moments of exquisite pain and sadness. But they are also moments of pure, complete love. It is because I so loved him that I still sometimes cry now, and that is a beautiful thing.

When you hit milestones, expected or unexpected, know the grief will be there. Just let it come; it flows through you like clean water.

Chapter Nine

TALKING TO DEAD PEOPLE

"I know this may come as a shock, and you know I'm not fond of using stale one-liners, but—'reports of my death have been greatly exaggerated.' I'm as alive now as I was on the day we met, except, maybe, more so."
—**Mike Dooley**, *The Top Ten Things Dead People Want to Tell You*

Am I Crazy Because I Talk to Him?

The other day I saw someone post in a Facebook group for widows asking, "Am I only one that talks out loud to my dead husband and do you think he hears me?"

I worried a little bit initially about wandering around my house, talking out loud to my dead husband. I worried what the neighbors would think if they could see in my window and see me walking around talking to no one. But the truth is, yes, I do talk out loud to Jim all the time. It's actually pretty common among widows to talk out loud to their husbands. One widow responded and said she spoke out loud to her deceased husband, especially when she was trying to do a task that he would normally have done. I get that. I've been there, done that.

You may have felt your faith falter after your spouse passed away, wondering why your beliefs and/or your god did not save him or leave him with you for more of your life together. Faith is quickly restored when you begin to pick up in so many small ways that your husband is not entirely gone. Do you wonder if he is "still there?" Is he just on the other side of time and space where he can see you and hear you?

I saw a spot of spilled coffee on the kitchen floor one night, and I laughed. I said out loud, "If you were still here, I'd blame you for that!" But "does he still hear me?" Wow, I think yeah—yeah, he does. Jim's presence was very palpable, especially in the early days right after he passed. Jim and I both had firm belief about life before birth and life after death. We wrote *Filomena's Fabulous Fable* together, back in those early days on the internet after we married. We had posted it to a discussion group that we were active in and also posted it to our home page back in the early 1990s. He and I wrote this together:

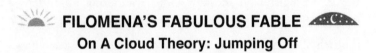 FILOMENA'S FABULOUS FABLE
On A Cloud Theory: Jumping Off

You're sitting on your CLOUD, blissfully paging through the ASTRAL ENQUIRER, occasionally glancing up as different Realities amble by. Suddenly, a tiny Blue Planet catches your eye. You sit up, the newspaper slips from your lap. You focus closer. You sense a situation coming together.

Something is happening! Your Soul is stirred—BANG!! You're hooked. A poor family in India? A Kennedy fantasy? Something in Tibet? A Moslem in Serbia? HOLLYWOOD? A blind child to be born? An Israeli Prime Minister?

You're standing on the edge of your CLOUD. There's an EXPERIENCE you must try! Love at first sight.

You check your astral watch. "Hey, I've got an hour before LUNCH!", you hear yourself say as you jump—joyfully streaking toward the Blue Planet.

QUESTIONS: FINAL EXAM

- When we arrive at the Blue Planet, why do we "seem" to forget why we jumped?
- Will you get back before Lunch?
- When you return to your CLOUD Reality, what will you remember?
- What insurance policies do I need?

- Does the newspaper carry advertisements? (Just kidding!)

Part of this story used to make me giggle: the thought that we would go back to lunch. With our group and our friends it became a common reference to talk about somebody going back to lunch, or when we go back to lunch. Jim, being diabetic, always said he couldn't wait to get back to lunch because he was going to have strawberry shortcake.

Signs and Symbols

So we had pretty solid belief that people are still around, before this life and after this life. He showed me this. There were times I felt that somehow, on a subconscious level, he knew before he passed away that this was it. Deep inside somewhere, he knew he was going to pass away before the end of that year. One of the things that gave me pause for thought: he was going into the hospital to have a stent put down in one of his legs. It was a "redo." He'd already had a stent put in his other leg. It was really no big deal. The morning that I was taking him there, he spotted a service vehicle across the street removing an oil tank from our neighbor's yard. He had a part of our yard that he wanted dug up, and it had been bugging him for a long time. So he ran over to find out if they would dig up that corner of our yard for us when they were done at our neighbor's and what they would charge for that. They kind of "old boy networked" across the street, and he came back just tickled pink because he felt he had a real good deal. When they were done, they were going to come over and dig up that one corner of our yard for us with their equipment so the soil would be all nice and turned for a new garden.

I remembered being worried at the time. The procedure to put a stent down his leg was supposed to be nothing. But I thought, "Wow, I think that must be the last thing bugging him that he had wanted done around the house for the yard. Is that like crossing off the last thing on his bucket list?" You know what? That was only about a month before he passed away. So it very well could have been just a matter of crossing off that last bit on his bucket list.

The day before he passed away, Jim sent an email to me. He had discovered Joe Cocker videos online, and he sent me one of Joe Cocker singing, "You Are So Beautiful to Me." A couple of weeks prior I had told him that my dad had never shared emotions. He used to call me a straw head. I later realized this was term of endearment from him because of my straw-color hair. But when I was little, I thought it was criticism because I had very long hair and would run like a wild little colt and play, and come home with my hair all tangled. I grew up thinking I was the ugly duckling daughter. It wasn't until I was 16 years old, after a situation that was frightening for all of us, that my dad said to me, "All I could think was my beautiful, beautiful daughter." I remember feeling stunned, crying, and saying, "You've never said that." I was touched that after sharing that story with Jim, he would send the music video to tell me I was beautiful—he wanted to make sure I knew I was not the ugly duckling little girl.

After he passed, I logged into his email to be able to do a group email to let everyone know he had passed. He had friends all over the country, and even in other countries, that he would exchange emails with about photography and various things. So I didn't want them left hanging. I got his distribution list to let them know what happened. I noticed in his email that the day before, when he had sent me "You Are So Beautiful" by Joe Cocker, he sent all his friends a link to Joe Cocker singing, "I Get By with a Little Help from My Friends." It gave me goosebumps. These were like parting gifts that he was sending out within a little more than 24 hours before he passed away.

After he passed away, did he hear me? Was he still around when I spoke to him? Oh, I definitely think so. One of the first indications was shortly after he had passed away when I was on the phone talking to his life-long friend, Glenn. They had both gone to the same grammar school in Queens. Jim still had the graduation book from St. Anthony's, and in it was a photograph of all of his buddies as little guys. About seven of these guys had stayed in touch their entire lives. We would annually get together with all of them for dinner.

Anyway, I was on the phone with Glenn and I went upstairs to pull the graduation book out because I wanted to ask Glenn if perhaps he would like to have it. I didn't know if he still had his copy of that photo with all of them. As I pulled it off the shelf at the top of the stairs while talking to Glenn, I suddenly got a very strong whiff of Old Spice aftershave. This was the aftershave Jim used because I loved it. There is still something about Old Spice that just gets to me. He knew that. He would put on aftershave, come downstairs and dance around me, sticking his neck down into my face, saying, "Does it do anything for ya?" So there I was with this sudden scent and wondering if in cleaning things out of the bathroom cabinet, I had spilled Old Spice. I didn't think anything more of it. I hung up after chatting with Glenn, and I thought, "Where did that smell come from?" I went back upstairs to find what it was that smelled of Old Spice. I checked the graduation folder, the rug, the bathroom. It was nowhere. There was no smell of Old Spice up there. It only came to me when I was talking to Glenn and looking at that old photo of them in the graduation folder. It was like he was sticking his neck down to my face saying, "What does it do for ya?" I was amused at the thought. The smell had been so distinct and so strong, there was no doubting it.

Further proof of faith: I had turned 60 in January, nearly a year before he passed. As part of my birthday, we paid to have roses of the month delivered so I would get roses every month of that year. I loved that! When the roses came for the month of December, I said to Jim, "Aw, these are my last roses!" He said, "You know we really should've arranged it so there would be one more bunch of roses delivered for your birthday again in January." I said that was okay, he could just buy me some flowers for my birthday. Of course that couldn't happen as he passed away December 29th. But could it?

On my birthday, I was down in the basement doing something. In the fall, I had brought in all the ceramic pots so they would not burst and crack in the freezing temperatures of winter. I had neglected to dump out a few of them because I just wanted to get them in, out of the cold. There, in a dark corner of the basement, was a pot with the remains of a fuchsia plant. It was completely dried out. It was so dry that the dirt had pulled away from the sides of the pot and the plant was just a mass of dead twigs. But I noticed there appeared to be leaves on it. When I went over and turned on the light to inspect it, I saw that it had sprouted. Not from the base of the plant, where you would expect a plant to "come back." It was sprouting from the ends of the dead branches. On one of those sprouts were two fuchsia buds. I couldn't believe my eyes.

I've always loved gardening and always pot up plants for the yard. I know some plants will come back after being stored if you keep them moist and you let them get some light. But I have never had any success, and this plant was completely dried out. The branches snapped off at a touch. There is no way it could've come back, especially not in mid-January. I brought it upstairs, gave it water and set it on the side of the sink where the sunlight could get to it, because there they were: two buds. And sure enough that plant blossomed. I chose to believe that Jim found a way to give me flowers for that next birthday.

Sure, many people will not believe that. But these are all little symbols and signs. You can miss even noticing them. You can write them off and say, "Oh it was just coincidence." It's how you chose to think about it and how you chose to feel about it. So when you speak to your dead spouse, do they hear you? Oh, I now know so. Read on.

Later that year, around early July, I received a final confirmation that Jim was still there. It was a beautiful evening. I was in a cotton nightgown, but I still slipped out back right at dusk to sit out on the patio where Jim and I used to sit together. I leaned back, looking up into our big old oak tree. I was wondering if he was there. I reached out in my thoughts, thinking, "When I think of you, when I talk to you, can you hear me? Do you come to me when I reach out to you?" I reached out with my thoughts as the sky darkened and the stars starting to come out. Suddenly I heard a neighbor slam shut a window and it brought me back out of my reverie. I looked down and realized that there on the patio, I was surrounded by fireflies. I hadn't seen any fireflies at all yet that summer. Usually we might see one or two in our backyard. I easily had two dozen fireflies around me. Fireflies were special to me, because growing up out in California, I had never seen them. After I moved to New York to marry Jim, we were taking a walk one evening through the Bronx and I started seeing some green flashes out of the corner of my eye. I thought I was having a stroke or something. Really! Why was I seeing these flashes of light? Finally I said something to Jim. I said, "I'm seeing these little green flashes! Are you seeing that? Is it just my eyes?" He said, "Oh, they're just fireflies." I was enraptured! Fireflies! I had never seen fireflies. He took a step back, drawing his hands up in pretend horror and said, "You *haven't*?" Then he was just overjoyed that he got to share fireflies with me for my first time. For the rest of that summer, every single evening, he would drag me out of our condo to walk through the park and go looking for fireflies.

This was absolutely not a coincidence that when I asked with all my heart, "When I think of you and talk to you and reach out for you, do you hear me? Do you come to me?" he came to me in a couple of dozen fireflies. You know, after that evening and for the rest of summer, I looked for fireflies and there were no fireflies in my yard or my neighbor's yard. It was not the kind of year that had the weather for there to be a lot of fireflies. I had never seen that many together at once before and I've never seen it since. It was just magic, that moment. It was my answer that yes, he hears me.

So talk to your dead spouse. Go ahead. You can tell them everything and anything. You may not get an impossible fuchsia. You may not get fireflies. But our loved ones are so there. When I spoke with Jim's sister shortly after he passed, she hesitantly told me that Jim was there with her the night that he passed away. She was very hesitant to tell me because she was afraid I would think she was a "crazy old lady." Dorothy said she had gone to bed and had put her head on the pillow, about to drift off, when she heard him say her name. She sat right up in bed and could sense his presence there. I told her by no means did I think she was a crazy old lady—Jim definitely would come to say good bye to his sister. They were incredibly close. Hearing your name is a phenomenon I experienced quite a few times after my father passed away. It has gone on for years. Occasionally I will hear my father's voice say my name right into my ear. It always makes me catch my breath, sit down, and think, "Okay, why is Dad getting my attention?" What am I doing here that I need to rethink?"

If you are paying attention, the dead will communicate with us in ways we may not expect. They show up in dreams. I expected a big dream from Jim at the very start! He used to do dream work. He believed strongly in the symbolism in dreams and did dream interpretation. He was excellent at dream interpretation—scary good at it. So when he first passed away and he wasn't coming to me in dreams, I was a little frustrated. I thought, wow man, dreams were your thing and you haven't come to see me in a dream yet? One night I demanded, saying, "You need to come to me in a dream. You need to let me know what's going on."

We had always talked about how, after you go back to lunch, you get to see the movies of your life. You get to see them from every viewpoint. Not just remembering your own viewpoint, but seeing them from other people's viewpoints. There would be things that you did in life that you had no idea the cosmic ripples you had sent out. One simple thing you said to a stranger may have changed their life. You wouldn't know it in this lifetime, but you get to find out when you see the movies after you get back to lunch.

That night, I got my dream. In the dream, I was walking through a house and I came around a corner. I could see all these luminous squares of light on the wall and these messy luminous handprints all over the wall. I thought, "What the heck?" Then I turned and saw Jim standing there. I thought, "I should've known. What are you doing? You're getting all these handprints on the wall!" He laughed, pointed to the wall and said, "Look!" When I looked back at the wall, all the squares became groups of photographs, like old Polaroid Instamatic shots on the wall. It made sense. Jim was a photographer and loved photography. He was dancing back and forth like a spritely elf and moving a photo from one group over to another group and getting all excited. He was shuffling them around, because he was making connections with these photos of things that were happening in this life that connected to something that happened in another life or time. It was fascinating. But when I woke up, my first thought was to be a little disappointed. I thought, "Wow, the afterlife is that low-tech? You didn't even get movies? You got pictures?" Then I started laughing. I realized that Jim would show me what he was accomplishing in the symbolism of photographs.

I was delighted he gave me that dream. He was doing pretty much what we had discussed. He was reviewing his life and all the connections, and he was having a hell of a good time doing it. It gave me joy and a renewed faith that he is still "there." I can talk out loud to him, and when the time comes that I slip from this earthly flesh, I'll see him again. We'll get to hug and catch up. I'll get to tell him all about the things I've done and learned since he left. That is a thought that gives me peace.

Chapter Ten

SETTING YOUR COURSE

"We can't become what we need to be by remaining what we are."

—Oprah Winfrey

Looking Ahead

Once you take all this in and learn how to process your grief, and even how your very thoughts create the emotions you experience, you begin to realize that your life is your responsibility. Up to now, you thought it was a shared responsibility with your spouse. But the truth is, it was really all yours all along. Because you can pay attention to your thoughts and ask yourself if the thought is really true. You can consider how a particular thought makes you feel, and then accept or pass over the thought if it is not supporting you. Now you begin to understand your own personal power. It is scary, but it is also exciting.

You may not be ready yet to set your course. The avalanche of emotions may feel overwhelming. I encourage you to find someone to talk you through this. Just because you are in emotional turmoil does not necessarily mean you need a prescription. But you do need a professional to guide you through. I highly recommend talking to a life coach. Yes, I am biased. But I'll tell you why. Traditional psychology takes you on a journey back through your past to identify what triggered your current emotional struggles. A life coach is trained to work with your thoughts and emotions at the very present and then move you forward from that point. Yes, experiences from the past come up. But it does not serve you to dwell there where nothing changes. Changes happen in the present, not in the past. When you work in the present, transformation can happen in an instant. I've seen this happen over and over.

When you are ready to consider the road ahead, it is time to consider what it is you want and why. Then imagine the goal happening and the outcome. How does it feel? Remember, emotions drive our actions. Everything we do is to feel a certain way or to avoid feeling a certain way. When you create a goal for yourself, you want to know how it feels to have that goal realized and tap into that emotion to drive your actions toward your goal. Ask yourself, "Do I truly believe I can achieve this outcome in my life?"

Goal setting is a spiritual practice. You might find that surprising because so many spiritual practices focus on being in the moment. But it is in the moment that you set and focus on what you want to create in your life. It is one of the most compassionate, wonderful things you can do for yourself. Having a goal, no matter how large or small that goal is, focuses the brain.

When your spouse passes away, your future feels nonexistent. Previous plans no longer make sense. No wonder you are wandering in a fog. The future is blank before you. All you see in that future is a continuation of the pain of your loss. It is time to begin to write a few small goals onto that blank slate. It is time to make a plan for yourself so you are not still sitting in the living room chair all day. The goal does not have to be practical. Allow yourself to dream a little. Maybe it is weight loss, maybe it is a new career, or spending time giving back to your community. Maybe you want to take up a long forgotten hobby again or travel somewhere.

Sometimes when you dream of something you would love to accomplish, it feels uncomfortable because you acutely feel the lack of it. Dreaming of it is reminding you of scarcity and the wanting of it. Don't stop dreaming, but dream of it as if it has already happened. Move beyond of that feeling of "wanting" to the feeling of "having." Dreaming should feel wonderful, not frustrating or painful.

A good place to begin goal setting is to return to the list of priorities you made back in chapter 3 about basic human needs. What were your top needs and how did you note that you might be able to get these needs met? Here are your first goals to set. Get those needs that are most important in your life met. If you do not create constructive ways to meet the needs that are important to you, you will certainly find destructive ways to meet those needs: smoking, drinking, sleeping in avoidance, overeating, or some other self-destructive behavior. It is a strong urge in our psyche to fill in the gaps in our needs.

Another way to get in touch with what you want is to brainstorm. Sit down with a tablet of paper and write down everything you want to do. *Everything.* Big dreams, outstanding chores, little tasks, crazy ideas. Keep writing without stopping until you can fill a page. Don't try to filter your thoughts and pick only what you think you *should* want. Just let it flow. Once you have your list, pick out the five things that are most important to you. Perhaps you will notice a couple of them are really the same outcome and they can be grouped together. Take each one and think about why you want to achieve it. What will it mean to you to achieve it? What will be the same in your life? What will be different in your life? Will you need to change a little as a person in order to make this happen?

Take your time to answer those questions. The answers will help you formulate your goals. Finally, you are going to want to list what you need to do to make those goals happen. Think about what obstacles you may face and list those. Next to each obstacle, plan a strategy to get around that obstacle. Lastly, give each goal a timeframe. One might only need a day to accomplish. Another might take a year.

Now you can plan the steps you need to take to complete your goals, and schedule each step onto your calendar. Commit to completing each small step on the day you've scheduled it.

Don't even think about the magnitude of trying to accomplish what you've set out for yourself. Just honor your commitment to the steps listed on your calendar. Then, like magic, your goal is completed. The real magic happens every morning when you open your eyes and know that you have a goal you are working toward that day. Offer up a "thank you" of gratitude for the day ahead of you that takes you one step closer. Allowing yourself to admit and commit to what you want becomes the navigation system of your soul, directing you to your destiny. Fear will come up, doubt will come up, maybe even shame or guilt. Just notice any thoughts you are having that drives those feelings. Write them down. Name them. You don't have to own them. Set those thoughts aside while you work toward your goal.

There is nothing that you genuinely want that you cannot have. What you truly desire is important information for you. It is what you are meant to have and accomplish for your very best self. It is what takes you through this mourning and brings you out into the light with the love for your spouse still intact, still living in your heart.

Chapter Eleven

AN AFTERWORD ON
AFTER LIFE AND LIFE AFTER

"Don't be dismayed at good-byes. A farewell is necessary before you can meet again. And meeting again, after moments or lifetimes, is certain for those who are friends."
—**Richard Bach**, *Illusions: The Adventures of a Reluctant Messiah*

Signs of Faith

J im did not want a funeral—he said they always made him vastly uncomfortable in life and he didn't want it in death because we both shared firm beliefs about the fact that we don't really "die" and disappear. Energy cannot just stop. It can transform and pass from one object to another (like playing billiards).

After my father passed away, his presence was very close for quite a while. He confirmed for me my early belief that we don't die in the traditional sense. I remember talking to him in the kitchen of my parents' house. He had an out-of-body experience when he clinically "died" in the hospital when he was in his 50s. A medication they had him on had slowed his heart too far, and it stopped. Code was called and his room full of medical staff trying to revive him. For some reason, the crash cart was not where it should have been—no paddles. A doctor jumped up onto my father, astride of him in his hospital bed, and punched him hard in the center of his chest. Dad took a breath and said, "Get the hell off of me." Music to that doctor's ears, I'm sure.

What no one knew until years later was that my dad, clinically dead, was out of his body and saw the entire episode. He was floating up by the ceiling, looking down on the entire scene. He told me, "When I saw that doctor jump on me and start punching me, it made me really mad—and I jumped back into my body and told him to get the hell off!" Laughable, yes. But it was also remarkable the things he relayed to me while my mother listened in stunned silence. It had happened years ago and he never told anyone.

I told dad what I believe about how we are really just energy using our earthly body for experiences, and that when we die, the energy does not just stop. We continue on, just without the body. I believed we were a lot like electricity. Then I said, "If you go before I do, I'm counting on you to let me know if I'm right or not!" Dad rolled his eyes comically, but nodded yes. We never talked about it again.

A few years later, there I was in a room at the local hospital where my father lay dying. The doctors had told us it was only a matter of time before he passed. It was Father's Day. We were all there taping up Father's Day cards around his bed where he now lay unconscious. At the end of that long day, suddenly all the lights went out on the floor of the hospital. There was shouting and rushing around in the hallway. Apparently it wasn't supposed to be able to happen—emergency backup generators are supposed to kick in immediately. It was apparently only on our floor of the hospital, so there was a lot of confusion about that. Really, the outage was only for minutes.

When the lights came back on, I looked down at Dad and knew. He was not breathing—he was gone. Medical staff were summoned and confirmed his death. But they didn't need to confirm it for me. Dad turned out the lights and turned them back on. He was telling me I was right: we are like electricity.

Others just patted me on the shoulder and said, "Well, I think it is just coincidence, Jo, as nice as it is to believe." Trust me. Over the ensuing days, they would *all* believe. On the day of his funeral, as my brothers, brother-in-law, and husband carried his casket out of the funeral home, the lights went out in the funeral home and came back on again. Everyone just looked over at me and shook their heads.

Dad was transported to Queen of All Saints Church for services. As my brothers again lifted his casket from the hearse and carried it into the church, the electricity went out in the church for a couple of minutes and came right back on again. At the end of the hour-long mass, as they carried his casket down the center aisle of the church to return to the hearse for the trip to the cemetery, the lights went out and came back on just as they exited the church with him. Nice job, Dad. Pretty damn spectacular.

Oh, and we had all been experiencing little things at home and at Mom and Dad's house and elsewhere. There were shared stories of a lot of lights going out and coming on again at key moments. My niece had a big armoire in her apartment that housed her TV and stereo equipment. Dad used to lecture her about leaving the doors open on it all the time, saying burglars could look in and see she had stuff to steal. She told me that every morning she was getting up and finding the doors closed on her armoire, when she knew darn well she did not do it. After a few days of this, it was so creepy that she started closing the doors on the entertainment armoire every night, "because it is too weird when Grandpa does it."

The final display was a week after my dad passed. My husband decided he needed to get me out to a movie or something to distract me from my grief. There was a new movie with Tom Cruise—he figured a Tom Cruise movie could certainly perk up my spirits. No doubt! So he swept me out of the house to go see *Far and Away*. What he didn't know was that the opening scene of the movie featured the sons standing around their father as he lay dying—then the camera panned up from the scene, denoting the father's soul leaving his body. My poor husband was doing a face/palm plant. But as the father died on the screen, the lights in the theater suddenly came back up on for a second and then dimmed back down again. As tears were streaming down my cheeks, I smiled, looked up and said, "Thanks, Dad." I was fine after that moment and enjoyed the movie.

Have you experienced such things? Don't be sad if you haven't. My brothers and sister and I all expected that Mom would haunt us after death. She was very psychic and we respected that. We couldn't get away with a darn thing! But after my mom passed away, I did not sense her presence as I had expected to, not at all like my dad's strong presence. For whatever reason, Mom just slipped right away. Maybe it was because Dad was waiting for her. Who knows?

Ashes

Jim was "around" after he passed, most noticeably the first three months or so. I knew his wishes about his ashes, and where he wanted them scattered. But I found I was not ready to do that immediately. Besides, it was frozen, snowy, and icy at the start of the New Year right after he died. We could not have gotten near the bridge and Esopus. I also still needed to sometimes sit on the stairs with the box of his ashes hugged to my chest. When my dear friend sent the hand-painted gourd as a tribute to him with peanuts inside for his squirrels, I did add a scoop of his ashes to the gourd and set it out in the snow under our giant oak tree that he so loved. He spent hours sitting out under that tree with our kitty cats and the squirrels. He was proud of the mighty oak and bragged about it. So I allowed his squirrels and nature to scatter a few of his ashes out under the oak. I knew he would like that. It also made the gourd decomposing and breaking down in the elements outside more meaningful for me as I imagined my own grief and pain also breaking down and disintegrating.

I finally decided his two sons and I should scatter his ashes on his birthday, April 12th. I made arrangements as the old bridge had long been closed to traffic and blocked off with chainlike fence. Before that day came, I took out a small tin box I had bought at a shrine in New Mexico the previous summer and filled it with a small scoop of his ashes—just so I would still have a bit of his ashes to hold near to my heart. Then we went out with the heavy box of his remains to take turns with the garden trowel, streaming his ashes down off the bridge into the river.

It was a setting he would have loved: Rural and in the trees, but nonetheless the bridge reminded me very much of the Bronx: gritty, fenced off, graffiti'd up a bit. The "No Trespassing" sign had been defaced. The entire activity felt just a tinge illicit. Yes, he would have loved that.

As I streamed a scoop of ashes over the side of the bridge, suddenly a tingling rush of energy entered my feet and whooshed right up my body, tingling all the way up. It was like ecstatic, gleeful energy rushing right through me. I quietly said to his sons, fully grown adult men standing on either side of me, "Did you feel that?" They both just turned and looked at me with huge eyes. There was my answer. Not only did they feel it, I think they were shocked to realize it was not just them.

I have since talked to others who have scattered the ashes of someone who passed on and had the experience confirmed as "mind blowing." Indeed, it was. I was very pleased because it seemed to me Jim was ecstatic over being released into his river—his energy streaming through the planet. Like his spirit was released to freedom.

Do I feel guilty that some of his ashes are under the oak and a few of his ashes in a small tin shrine box here with me? Not at all. Jim would understand. He would be pleased. Someday that small tin of ashes may go back down to the Bronx with me, either to the Bronx River or to Our Lady of Lourdes Grotto at St. Lucy's, which he loved. St. Lucy's is the place of the miracle of a spring of healing waters that took place in the Bronx. But for now, those last bits of ashes still remain here with me. It is taking care of what I need as I move through this journey of healing back to finding who I am now.

So whatever it is you choose to do, let there be no guilt. I know for many it is a traditional funeral and internment within days of their loved one's passing and probably you were in a fog pretty much through the entire experience. No matter. It is what is, and it all happens exactly as it should. No guilt, no remorse for those decisions and preparations. Guilt and remorse do not serve us. What serves us is the love we still feel for them, and that is what should remain in its purest form.

Finding Your Sign

If you feel that there have been no "signs" of your spouse, realize that you may not be looking or even accepting of such things. I had a girlfriend whose fiancé passed away. Their beliefs about reality and death were the same as Jim and I. A few nights after he passed, there had been a huge explosion down on an overpass near her that lit up the entire night sky. No one was hurt; no one died. It was reported as a miracle that lives had not been lost in that horrible explosion of a tanker. A week later she was lamenting to me that he had not sent a sign at all. She couldn't believe he would pass away and not send her a sign! I said, "Are you kidding? Didn't he just recently light up the entire night sky for you?" The stunned look on her face was priceless and we both dissolved into laughter. There were many other little things, all of which she had overlooked because she just was not seeing what was.

Another widow friend finds hearts constantly from her deceased spouse. She knows to look for them, and they turn up all over the place. Heart-shaped rocks, heart-shaped leaves, hearts in the clouds, a flower with a deformed center that should have been perfectly round, but instead had bloomed into a heart. A knot in the wood of a table, shaped in a heart. The center of a strawberry; an imperfect tomato. He constantly sends her love.

Do you know where to look? Have you been overlooking the odd cardinal in your yard? The impossible blossoms on a dead plant? Just be assured that even if you do not see it, our loved ones are there—looking in on us, waiting for the day we join them and get to sit down and celebrate our lives we had shared together.

Chapter Twelve

THE BEGINNING

"Well, if it can be thought, it can be done, a problem can be overcome,"

  —**E.A. Bucchianeri**, *Brushstrokes of a Gadfly*

Obstacles in the Road

Widows will always tell you that the second year is worse than the first. I believe this is actually the journey moving forward and may not indicate specifically year number two, but rather how life feels after you move through that first year of being self-protected in a fog and getting extra attention and help from family. Now you will begin to become aware of the obstacles along the way. You are still in a heightened state of stress. This chapter is going to talk about just a few of the obstacles from the first year and moving forward.

Drs. Thomas Holmes and Richard Rahe created the "Social Readjustment Rating Scale" in 1967. This scale is used to assess a number of "units of stress" to each type of life change event. A high number on the scale indicates the need for professional assistance from a trusted doctor or talking to a counselor or life coach. I found a copy of a worksheet for adult assessment by The Kent Center for Human & Organizational Development. The units on this scale are fascinating to me. On the low end is a minor violation of the law, like a traffic ticket. That is five units. It goes up from there, listing many small stressors. Taking out a minor financial loan is ten units, chronic allergies 20 units, your spouse out of work is 20 units. It jumps higher with foreclosure of mortgage at 25 units, work change at 35 units, fired at work at 45 units, and the death of a family member who is not your spouse at a whopping 60 units. At the very top of the scale is the death of your spouse: 100 units.

What does this mean for you? Consider that your spouse's death is probably going to also include a financial change and that is 38 units. Revision of personal habits is 24 units. Change in social activities is 18 units. Change in living conditions is 25 units. Already you are at 205 units—far more than anyone can handle during the course of a year. The recommendation is to seek help at that high a number. Add in sleeping less than eight hours, and you tack on another 25 units to 230 units! This is why my life coaching business has taken on a new "specialty" and I have begun focusing on working with widows in need of life coaching. I know the emotional pain firsthand, and I understand the level of stress and the obstacles you encounter.

The widow is a changed person and goes through a long period of inner anger, bitterness, and confusion. If you have made new friends as a widow, bless those friends because they have befriended you when you are not at your best. You've not exactly been yourself. Can you say, "Widow Pass, please?" I have never been insecure, frightened, constantly sizing up situations, or feeling inferior like this before. But scoring over 200 on the stress scale over the course of a year will do this. Not to mention the brain fog due to the stress level. I went through a year of no longer being able to remember names and I still struggle with this.

Here is the short list of obstacles you need to be aware of:

- Social isolation. Unbelievably, there seems to be a plunge in social status for a widow, even in the face of the enlightened feminism of today's world.
- Servant status. You are alone with nothing more in your life, so employers take unfair advantage of your time. Friends take unfair advantage of your time based on the assumption that you are always home and would be glad to baby sit or pet sit, or pull the extra shift or answer phones through the evening. You have no husband, no family, so why not?
- Minority group: "women without men." That's right; you've just joined a minority club of widows.

- Family treating you like a child and stepping in to "help run your life." They are well-meaning and acting out of love, but they overstep and belittle you in the process.

- The opinions of others on the length of your visible grief. Too short and it will raise an eyebrow, with friends perhaps telling each other," She must not have loved him very much." Too long and your grief makes them uncomfortable and they wish you would get over it.

- Memories at every turn. Just when you think you are fine, you open a drawer and see one item that triggers a wash of tears and memories.

- Your work can give you focus and respite from grief during the day, but when you return home each evening, your grief is right there, waiting on your doorstep.

- Fear: economic fear, fear of being alone forever.

- Weight gain or loss—or both!

- Loneliness: feeling like you're wandering in the wilderness.

- Uncharacteristic anger. Still, after all those days of grief, you're triggered, furious, and lashing out at others. In truth, you are angry that your spouse died, but it can translate into all kinds of expressions of anger and bitterness.

The list can go on and on. But the point is, you are not alone in any of this. Don't be embarrassed by any of this or feel guilty about any of this. Seek help. Getting help to talk through your grief and the obstacles along the way can help you immediately begin to feel better and move forward in your grief and in your life.

Be very careful with Facebook groups for widows. Just "liking" a page that is not monitored closely can open you to all kinds of unsavory "friend requests" on Facebook. Don't be completely afraid of Facebook—I love Facebook and have my life coaching page there and a page for *Widow Cast*, my podcast. But do use caution when accepting friend requests. I "joined" a widow group on Facebook that was not a "hidden, private group" and suddenly was bombarded with friend requests from men who appeared to have fake profile pages. Usually there was a picture of a good-looking gentleman hugging a little girl in a park or with a young boy, to show they are a "family" man. Those photos were nothing short of creepy. Not much information. Career is usually listed as something unbelievable like a rocket scientist in France or an air force officer, or having studied abroad at Glasgow University. These are not real people, and they are stalking widows. It is unfortunate, but it exists.

Grief groups can be helpful but also frustrating, as they usually attract a mixed bag of attendees from widows to kids who have lost parents or parents or have lost kids. I have had clients share thoughts with me that they have told me they could not even bring themselves to share in their grief group! If you are going to attend a grief group, it needs to be a place where you feel complete safe and comfortable sharing. This is why working one-on-one with someone is often preferable. You can feel safe and open up to a trusted professional.

My podcast, *Widow Cast,* is on iTunes, Stitcher and on Google Play Music. It is free to download and listen to the episodes. I also have a download sheet you can get from my website for the Holmes Stress Points Scale. Look for the download link on my books page at http://Joannbooks.com. Enter your email address and I will email the information sheet and a worksheet of questions to answer to assess how you are doing.

WIDOWED

As you move ahead in your life, remember the lessons I've shared here along the way.

W *Widow Pass*—Find what makes you happy and do that. Forgive yourself for the small omissions, misplaced papers, and even dancing naked. You have a Widow Pass.

I *Identify Your Basic Needs No Longer Being Met*—Find ways to ensure those needs continue to be met in a positive, constructive manner.

D *Do It at Your own Pace*—This journey is unique to each one of us.

O *Omit the Guilt*—Your grief is separate from guilt, and is beautiful

W *Widow to Widow Connection*—Reach out to another widow, as you will truly understand how the other feels.

E *Each Day*—Live each day as if this year is your last year to live. Find joy in every day, no matter how small.

D *Dare to Dream*—Yes, you experience emotional trauma, but this can also inspire you to reach for tremendous personal growth. It is through this that you find out who you really are and learn just how strong you really are.

You have a Widow Pass! You will remain in a fog; respect that protective layer and don't expect yourself to be perfect. Find what makes you happy. With those new widow eyes that now understand the value in every day of life, make the most of your life. Live every single day as if it were your last. If you wake up in the morning and are dreading what you are going to be doing that day, it is time for a change. Make sure you are getting your priority needs met! Put yourself into #1 position. You get to do this on *your* schedule and in the order and way that you need to process your grief. There is not set order or timeline. Every widow is going to be different. Get out there and initiate contact with friends, and make some new friends. They are not going to come to you as you sit frozen in your living room. It can be very hard to find the motivation to get out. But you need human contact.

Don't confuse grief with all the other emotions that are going to come up with it, especially guilt! You can choose the thoughts you focus on. If you're feeling guilty, what are you thinking and is it true? Know that those "widow moments" can come out of nowhere. Honor your grief. Dare to dream again. Allow the shock, pain, and traumatic stress to become your catalyst for personal growth. Begin the spiritual practice of setting goals and assigning a timeline to them. Take the steps to make your goals and dreams a reality. You may not feel ready for this yet. There may be entire chapters that sound too optimistic to even consider. But the time will come when you are ready. When it does, read this book again and even reach out to me. This is your beginning, not your end. Get out there and find joy in your life.

FURTHER READING

A Year to Live: How to Live This Year as If It Were Your Last, by Stephen Levine

The Power of Intention: Learning to Co-create Your World Your Way, by Dr. Wayne W. Dyer

The Top Ten Things Dead People Want to Tell You, by Mike Dooley

Illusions: The Adventures of a Reluctant Messiah, by Richard Bach

Oprah's Saving Gracie, by Oprah Winfrey, *O Magazine* August 2007 Issue

What Doesn't Kill Us: The New Psychology of Posttraumatic Growth, by Stephen Joseph

Awaken the Giant Within, Tony Robbins

ACKNOWLEDGMENTS

It has been my honor to have known and coached widows who freely opened their hearts to me to share their pain, fears, and hopes. Without them, this book could not have been written. Without them, my podcast would have never become a reality. Each review and recommendation I have received from them has moved me to tears. I deeply appreciate the widows who have reached out to other widows to share a pat on the back, a hug, support, and friendship.

Of course, none of this would have happened without some amazing mentors who have become a part of my life along the way. Special thanks to Brooke Castillo, CEO of The Life Coach School, for giving so freely of herself to her coaches and to the world. It was the tools of life coaching that helped me move forward in my new life. Thanks to Angela Lauria, Publisher at Difference Press, for grabbing my hands into hers, looking me right in the eye, and saying, "You must write that book." Angela never let go of my hands as I wrote and created the book you now hold in your hands. Without her belief in my inner author, it would not have been possible.

Lastly I want to thank my greatest mentor and teacher for over 20 years who gave me the gift of who I am today: Jim Filomena. There exists so much of us in each other after all those years of shared books, tapes, discussions, and adventures. One thing we shared with absolutely certainty was our love and the knowledge that we create our own reality—there is no other rule. I can't wait to catch up with you again "back at lunch" so we can talk about all that has transpired since your death. Have the strawberry shortcake ready for me.

Love, Joann

ABOUT THE AUTHOR

Professionally certified Life Coach and Weight Loss Coach Joann Filomena speaks widow to widow, having walked this path herself after the sudden loss of her husband. A California girl turned New Yorker and now living in the heart of the beautiful Hudson Valley, she is the producer and host of *Widow Cast* and *Weight Coach* podcasts, each with listeners spanning the globe. Joann uses her life experience and coaching skills to help her clients through widowhood, weight loss, and many other life issues that arise in those sessions, all with incredible authenticity and compassion.

As a Life Coach, she has seen profound, seemingly impossible transformations in clients. The new widow who felt all her life plans pulled out from under her on the death of her husband, now moving ahead in her life with direction and purpose. Widows who feared they could not live alone finding how much they can savor and thrive in their very own space. The widow who could not even get out of bed most mornings and now looks forward to each new day. Joann constantly reminds us that we can all move forward after loss into tremendous personal growth, even as we carry those we've lost in our hearts.

THANK YOU

Thanks for reading WIDOWED. I'd love to hear about your journey through widowhood. Please email me or comment on Facebook on the page for the *Widow Cast* podcast: **www.facebook.com/widowcast/**

My email is **Joann@JoannTheLifeCoach.com**

Visit my website at **JoannTheLifeCoach.com**

As a special thank you, I invite you to download the Holmes Stress Point Scale and question worksheet to go along with the book, for free. Just go to this link and enter your email address so I can get it to you: **Joannbooks.com**

Last but certainly not least, I invite you to download and listen to my podcast for widows. I had always loved listening to podcasts, so it was no surprise that after my spouse passed, I went searching in iTunes to hear something, anything from another widow. At that time, there was not one podcast for widows. It was in my heart to do this podcast and so, a year later, I made it a reality. It is free to download, listen, and subscribe! **joannthelifecoach.com/widowcast**

Morgan James
Speakers Group

✦ www.TheMorganJamesSpeakersGroup.com

We connect Morgan James published
authors with live and online events
and audiences whom will benefit
from their expertise.